one & two color graphics

two

P·I·E Books

one & two color graphics

Copyright ©1997 by P·I·E Books

All rights reserved. No part of this publication may be reproduced in any form or by any means, graphic, electronic or mechanical, including photocopying and recording by an information storage and retrieval system, without permission in writing from the publisher.

P·I·E Books
Villa Phoenix Suite 301, 4-14-6 Komagome, Toshima-ku, Tokyo 170 Japan
Tel:03-3940-8302 Fax:03-3576-7361
e-mail: piebooks@bekkoame.or.jp

ISBN 4-89444-040-7 C3070 P16000E

First published in Germany 1997 by:
NIPPAN / Nippon Shuppan Hanbai Deutschland GmbH
Krefelder Straße 85, D-40549 Düsseldorf, Germany
Tel:0211-5048080/89 Fax:0211-5049326

ISBN3-910052-91-6

Printed in Hong Kong

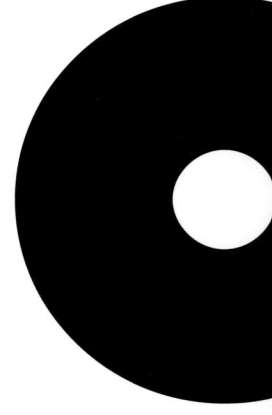

contents

introduction	4
posters	10
printed material brochures, flyers, direct mail	55
publications books, magazines, newsletters	128
stationery letterheads, envelopes, business cards	154
packaging product packaging, shopping bags, cd jackets	167
others calendars, 3-dimensional items, co-ordinated materials	182
index of submittors	217

イントロダクション

『1色＆2色デザイン』ということについて、6人のデザイナーの方に自由にコメントしていただきました。共通していたのは、色数の限定という一見ネガティブな条件を制約とは考えず、様々な可能性を追求する場としてポジティブにとらえている点でした。

『2色＞4色』 Cyan

サイアンの活動は文化的な分野に限られています。予算が限られているからということもありますが、これらのプロジェクトにおいては、手の込んだ複製技術やリトグラフ、4色印刷は過去のものとなりつつあります。そこで私たちは1色＆2色印刷のあらゆる可能性を追求し、色々な実験を試みます。またこの限られた方法で制作することは、私たちにとっては美的探究という意味でもやりがいがあります。加えてこれは環境保護の側面からも重要であり、フィルム、印刷版、化学薬品などを節約したり、適切な印刷用紙を選ぶことは大切なことです。私たちの考えでは、『リアルさ』を『完璧』に再現し、紙の上にコピーして人々を過剰に刺激するという方法は、もはや無効になっています。ハイテクイメージの外交員が登場するあらゆる保険会社のケバケバしたパンフレットや、『我が家こそ我が城』的な住宅金融組合の雑誌に描かれたイラストは、美的・技術的に可能な方法を使い尽くしてしまいました。私たちはこのような観点から出発し、内容・官能性・本質的美を統合する方法と、また、時間が経った後も鮮やかに記憶に残るようなデザインの手法を捜し求めています。さらに過剰な科学薬品を使用しなくてすむ素材も探しています。天然紙では色の写りや印象が違ってくるので、デザイン表現の組み立てを変える必要があります。クライアントとのブリーフィングの中でこうした諸々の問題について議論するのですが、なかなか理解してもらえないこともあります。予算が限られているにも関わらず、クライアントはカラフルで光沢のあるものを求めることが多いのです。私たちはこれまでに、天然紙の上で2色を混ぜ合わせたり塗り重ねたりすることを随分くり返してきましたが、これは今なお実に興味深い実験であり、最終的な色は印刷機にかけた時に決まるのです。

オフィスプロフィール：サイアン
「サイアンの創作物はそのコンセプトにおいて、1920年代から30年代初期にかけてのアヴァンギャルドデザインを志向するものであり、また見る者に知覚・経験する能力を開発する機会を提供する視覚的文化を提案するものです。（中略）サイアンは写真を巧みに合成し組み合わせる手法を自在に駆使し、多用します。しかしながら同様に、最新の表現環境の中で古き良きボドニを取り入れたり、文化的伝統から美的緊張を生み出したり、テクストとイメージと紙を融合させてファーストフード広告戦略に対抗しうる独自の存在物を創り出す能力も持ち合わせます。」J. ペトルシャット博士ーノヴム誌（ドイツ・デザイン誌）／94年2月

『見慣れたものを見慣れないものへ』 Sean O'Mara

自分の個性を商業デザインの中でいかに表現するかという私の考え方は、記号論を学んだ時に根底から覆されました。何よりもまず、組み合わせが意味と解釈を定義するということに気づいたのです。日常的にデザイナーが使用するグラフィック言語（対象／紙／イメージ）をまったく新しい視覚的組み合わせの中で使うことが、見慣れたものを見慣れないものへ変える方法であり、また自分の中にある強烈なイメージをデザインの中で表現する1つの方法になりました。

本書に掲載されている私の作品は、視覚的な組み合わせを弄び、日常見慣れているはずの要素で、まったく新しい別の意味を伝えようとしています。つまり、通り一遍の意味の中で生活している人々の中に驚きや違和感が生じれば、私の意図したことは100％達成できたと言えます。

商品を魅力的に見せようとする言葉（つまり広告）は、受け手を引きつけ、"思考"を喚起するものであって欲しいものです。

グラフィックデザインとは、言葉と絵によってアイデアを視覚的に結びつけ、消費者のニーズを明確に表現しようとするものです。多くの場合商業デザイナーは、テーマを与えられるとそれに沿った要素を集め、テーマに最も合うように、時に冒険的に組み合わせます。しかしながら、一方的にアイデアを伝えてモノを売ろうとすることに終始し、相手から何かを引き出そうとすることはありません。デザインすることの最終的な目的は、見る者に思考を喚起させ、メッセージを理解させることであり、かつ作品に個性を持たせることにあります。受動的にではなく、主体的に見させることがグラフィックデザイナーの仕事なのです。

プロフィール：ショーン・オマラ
1967年オランダ生まれ。1985-90年 ダンレアラ・カレッジ・オブ・アート・アンド・デザイン（ダブリン）卒業。1990年 Xon Corpデザインスタジオ（ダブリン）設立。1991-93年 セントラル・セントマーティンズ・カレッジ・オブ・アート・アンド・デザイン（ロンドン）卒業／修士号取得。1993-95年 イマジネーション社（ロンドン）シニアデザイナー。現在、ボディ・ショップ・インターナショナル（ロンドン）でシニアデザイナー兼マネージャーを務める。

『メッセージを色で伝えるということ』 Stoere Binken Design

私たちは1色または2色の制作を楽しんでいることが殆どです。なぜならフルカラー印刷では失われがちな美的純粋性や抽象性を持たせることができるからです。もちろん1＆2色の作品にはクライアントの資金を大幅に節約するという、もう1つの（同じように重要な）側面もあります。このことが限られた刷り色で制作する主な理由であることも少なくありません。

2色で制作する場合、色の彩度を思いどおりにコントロールすることができます。2色のかけ合わせによりたくさんの色のグラデーションを作ることができます。このようにして平面でありながら緻密に層をなす作品を作り出し、作品に独特の雰囲気を生み出し、見るものの感情に訴えかけます。

こうやって色の試行錯誤を続けると'良いデザイン'の核心に触れられそうになります。一それは、伝えようとするメッセージが非常にストレートで、しかも嘘がなく、かつ奥行きがあるということです。優れたデザインとは美しいだけのものを作ることではなく、クライアントの意図にかなうグラフィック言語を生み出すことなのです。

残念なことですが、最近の著しいマルチメディアブームにおいては、デザインはごまかし的に現れてはすぐ消えるフルカラーイメージとなり、もはや人目を引く以外の能力が無くなりつつあるように思います。この過程でメッセージが押し潰されてしまうことが非常に多いのです。

オフィスプロフィール：ストーレ・ビンケン・デザイン
オランダのマーストリヒトにある比較的若いグラフィックデザインスタジオ。親友である2人から成る。アカデミー・オブ・ファイン・アーツ・マーストリヒトを卒業後すぐに活動を始める。国内外においてさまざまなクライアントを持ち、内容はCI、CDジャケット、雑誌、フライヤーなど多岐に渡る。「私たちはデザインに対して独自のビジョンを持っています。だからクライアントは私たちを選んでくれるのです。」

『2色であることの理由』 Darin Beaman

私たちの仕事の60％以上は、1色ないし2色しか使用していません。これはアートセンターが非営利の学術団体で、予算が限られているためです。予算が限られるとデザインも制約を受けると考えると人もいますが、私たちはいかなる印刷物も私たちの視覚言語を開発し、発展させる良い機会であると考えています。

例えば本書に掲載されている『Objects』展カタログです（P132）。この展覧会は出展作品数も予算も多くはありませんでしたが、テーマはとても高尚で、私たちに完全にオリジナルな解答を求める命題のようでした。このカタログの形態はオブジェとしての本を表現しています。綴糸とチーズクロスを露出させて、製本過程の一部としての物質性を強調しました。ハードカバーをはずし、各本文ページには表紙と同じ紙を用いて、本の「非具体化」ということに徹底しました。こうして、本と単なるモノとの境界線を微妙に混乱させたわけです。

このような小規模のプロジェクトでは、既成の概念に捕らわれない自由な発想が必要とされます。私たちはこのようなプロジェクトにとてもこだわります。なぜなら、こうした手法が私たちを未知の方向へ、また新しい方法論へと導いてくれるかもしれないからです。

オフィスプロフィール：
1986年、アートセンター・カレッジ・オブ・デザイン学長デーヴィッド R. ブラウン氏がデザインオフィスを設立。カレッジのすべての印刷物を担当。1987年以降、副学長兼クリエイティブディレクター、スチュアート・フロリック氏がデザインオフィスを管理している。1991年、カレッジ専属デザイナー、ダリン・ビーマン氏が加わる。本書の掲載作品は、2人のアートディレクターと5人のデザイナー、プロジェクトのための制作スタッフにより5年がかりで制作されたもの。

『色の記憶』 Jean-Benoît Lévy

今これを読んでいるあなたは、何色が好きですか？私の好きな色はその時の気分や、たぶん季節によっても変わります。

昼、夜、そして移ろいやすい光の中で、色は常に自己主張し、その周囲にあるものと対立しています。デザインにおいては、写真やタイポグラフィの選択と同様に色の選択は最も重要です。色はその色が発する雰囲気と共に存在します。これが分かれば問題はもはや「なん色使うか？」ではなく「どの色を使うか？」になります。

バーゼルの劇場ポスターシリーズを制作した時は、私はまず初めに実際の作品を読み、デザインと劇の内容が調和するようにしました。私は作家が作品の初めに特定の場所（街、森）・時間（朝、夜...）・背景（家の中、屋外）を示し、1つまたは複数の色を仄めかす場合が多いことに気づきました。

また、私は常に、自分の周囲にあるもの、自分の目に映るものの影響を素直に受け入れるようにしています。ーファッション、他の人のグラフィックデザイン、斬新なフライヤー、そして自然の中の、あるいは画筆を洗っている時に偶然に生まれる面白い色のコンビネーションなどです。私はこのような「視覚の決定的瞬間」を重要だと感じ、この「色の記憶」を意識し、忘れないように努めます。

アートディレクションが定まった後も色はなお発展し続け、製作時まで続くことさえあります。最終的に色調・明度・濃度・彩度が決まるのはプレスチェックの時です。そして完成したポスターが街に貼られているのを見た時に、やっとその色の選択が正しかったかどうかが分かるのです。

今日あなたはどんな色の組み合わせを身につけますか？よく選んでください。色はあなたの個性を反映することもあるのですから！

プロフィール：ジャン＝ベノワ・レヴィ
1959年生まれ。1978－83 デザイン・カレッジ（バーゼル）卒業。1983－86 スイス・フェア（見本市）にてデザイン担当。1987 ローザンヌにて定期誌2誌のエディトリアル・デザイン担当。同年6か月間フリーランス。1988 And, Trafic Grafic 設立。1991年以降、アートセンター・カレッジ・オブ・デザイン・ヨーロッパ、デザイン・カレッジ（バーゼル）、アメリカのRISDにて講師を担当。現在はデザイン／広告の分野にとらわれず活躍。最近ではスイスPTTの切手をデザインする。

『デザインのウラのデザイン』 Makoto Orisaki

おもに色数の制約は予算によるものだろうが、私はそれらがクリエイティブの制約にならないことの実践として、絵柄のデザインを越え、分野外素材やミシン目などの特殊加工を施している。この場合には仕入から物流、技術、そして理解ある工場（職人）のセッティングとコスト設計がすべてである。本来のグラフィックデザインの外にあるもののようだが、この作業無くしては実現しない。その結果として予算内での新たな試みや、異業種間の交流がなされている。

日本人の紙に対する質感、価値観を問う意味も含め、数年前から産業用紙（板紙、ボール紙etc.）を使ったデザインを試みている。マルチメディアでは今のところ表現できないリアルな情報である触感、質感は紙媒体の重要点ととらえている。日本の印刷用紙は印刷適正にとらわれすぎた画一的な紙が多く、もっと表情豊かな紙（再生紙）があって欲しいと考える。自ら開発生産にかかわれたらと考え、実体験のマーケティングとして、ＤＭ作りを最も有効な実験の場としている。最近では製造・再生・美的にも有利であると考え、究極の０色デザインを仕掛けている。

プロフィール：織咲 誠
1965年生まれ「デザインで"自己表現する"ということには全く興味ない。ただいつも気に留めているのは『ヒューマンエラー』というコト。何かを形にし、社会に出すという行為はあらゆるもの（価値観や文化、生活etc.）に対してなにがしかの影響を与えることになりうるので、責任ある立場をとりたい。デザインするということは、洞察眼を持ち、すべて（機能、心身、環境、美、ユーモアetc.）に対してベストな状態を導き出す行為と考えている。そのようにして生み出されたものは、必然として個を越える。」

INTRODUCTION

As an introduction to this collection, we offer here the comments of six designers on the subject 'design with one or two colors'. They share the view that a limitation on the use of color should be seen not as a handicap, but as an opportunity offering a wealth of potential to explore.

"two > four" cyan

cyan works exclusively in the cultural sector. for these low and no budget projects, the question of elaborate reproduction techniques, lithography and 4c printing is mostly obsolete. thus we try to use all possibilities of one and two colour printing and to experiment with these. moreover it is aesthetically interesting for us to work with these minimal means. in addition, the ecological aspect is important. we consider it important to save film material, printing plates, chemicals etc. and to use adequate printing paper... the over stimulation with <<perfectly>> reproduced and printed <<reality>> is in our opinion used up. high-tech quality of images for the employees of any insurance broker in a glossy ad brochure or the illustrations for a <<my-home-is-my-castle>> building society magazine have overstrained the technical and aesthetical possibilities. starting from this point we look for solutions which are a unity with regard to content, sensuality and aesthetics and which do not wear off or disappear after one single brief glance. moreover we look for materials which exclude the use of superfluous chemicals. natural papers ask for a different style of work on images as colours print and look differently. during briefing, all this is discussed with the clients who are sometimes not easily convinced. often they want, in spite of limited finances, something colourful and glossy. even though we have plenty of experience in mixing and layering two colours on natural paper, it still remains a most interesting experiment, and the final colours are fixed at the printing machine.

Office profile: cyan
"cyan describes its conceptual planning as traditionally slanted toward the design avant-garde of the twenties and early thirties, as proposal for a visual culture in which the individual's ability to perceive and experience is given a chance to develop. [...] this explains its preference for photography, its masterful manipulation of montage and dissolve techniques. but there's also the ability to include good old bodoni in a completely new expressive environment, to transform cultural traditions into aesthetic tensions, to weld text, image and paper into a single entity that can stand up against fast food ad ploys." by dr. j. petruschat in novum (german design magazine) 2/94

"Communicating the client's message through colour" Stoere Binken Design

More than often we prefer to work with one or two colours because it gives an aesthetic purity and abstraction to the artwork that you often lose with full colour printing. Of course, another (no less important) aspect of one & two colour work is that it saves the client lots of money. Many times this is the main reason for working with limited colours.

Working with two-colour artwork gives you total control over the intensity of the colour. The fusion of two colours produces other colours that can be varied into numerous gradients. In this way you can create densely layered artwork that is less 2-dimensional, that creates an atmosphere and stimulates the emotions of the viewer.

Experimenting with colour in this way brings us closer to what good design is all about; communicating the message in a very direct, honest and profound way. Good design is not about making beautiful things, but creating a graphic language that serves the intentions of the client.

Unfortunately, the recent multimedia explosion has set the decor for designs with flashing, rapidly changing full colour images that are merely used to get the viewer's attention. Too often the message is suffocated in this process.

Office profile: Stoere Binken Design
We are a relatively young graphic design studio, stationed in Maastricht, the Netherlands. Our studio consists of two good friends. We started off directly after graduating from the Academy of Fine Arts Maastricht. We operate on an (inter)national level and have a variety of clients. Our work varies from corporate identities, CD sleeves, to magazines, flyers, etc. We have our own vision about design and that's why clients choose us.

"The Object of Two Colors" Darin Beaman

More than 60 percent of the projects at Art Center are one- or two- color. This is due to the limited budgets in a nonprofit academic environment. Some think that these limitations also limit the design, but we see any printed piece as an opportunity to develop and expand our visual language.

An example of this is the *Objects* exhibition catalog (pg.132), which is featured in this volume. The quantity and budget were small, but the subject matter was rich; it seemed to demand a unique solution. The form of the catalog addresses the notion of the book as object. We exposed the binding threads and cheesecloth to emphasize their materiality as part of the book production process. We stripped the catalog of its hard cover and used cover stock for the text pages, continuing the strategy of "dematerializing" the book. These elements were combined to create a subtle category confusion between book and object.

We are compelled to take risks and explore unconventional conceptual and production options on smaller projects. We remain committed to their every detail because we never know where they will take us—or what new thinking they may inspire.

Office profile: Design Office for Art Center College of Design
Founded in 1986 by President David R. Brown, Art Center's Design Office is responsible for all the college's printed material. Stuart Frolick, vice president and creative director, has supervised the office since 1987. Designer for the College Darin Beaman joined Art Center in 1991. The work represented in this volume was completed over a five-year period by two art directors, five designers, and a limited production staff.

"Remembrances of Colors"
Jean-Benoît Lévy

What's your favorite color, you who are reading this text? Personally, mine changes according to my mood or maybe the season.

By night, day and in any type of light a color is constantly in confrontation with its surroundings. Just as photography and typography, the selection of color is essential. Colors exist by the feelings they exude. Once this is determined, the question is no longer, "how many colors?", but "which colors?".

In the case of the theater poster series I created for Basel, I first read the actual works before starting so that my design would correspond to the performed pieces. I found that authors often begin their texts by indicating specific location (a town, a forest), a time of day (morning, evening...), a setting (in a house, outdoors) and allude to one or more colors.

I also allow myself to be influenced by what I see around me: fashion, other graphic designs, innovative flyers, interesting combinations in nature and even accidentally when washing out my paint brushes. Aware of the importance of these "visual moments", I try to hold on to "remembrances of colors".

After an artistic direction is taken, the colors still continue to evolve, even up until production. It is with the printer on the presscheck that the last decisions of tone, transparency, deepness and saturation are made. And later, when I see the poster hung out in the street, I can finally see if the color choices were the right ones.

What colors will you wear today? Choose them well because they may also be the reflection of your personality!

Profile: Jean-Benoît Lévy
Born 1959. Schule für Gestaltung (College for Graphic Design), Basel 1978-1983. Graphic designer at Schweizer Mustermesse (Swiss Trade Fair) 1983-1986. Magazine designer for two periodicals in Lausanne, summer 1987. Freelancer in San Francisco for six months, 1987. Foundation of own studio "And, Trafic Grafic", summer 1988. Lecturing at Art Center College of Design Europe 1991-1996 and at Schule für Gestaltung, Basel 1993-1994. Guest lecturer at Rhode Island School of Design, Providence, USA, winter 1995-1996. Current work encompasses the complete spectrum of graphic design and advertising. Has just produced a postage stamp for the Swiss PTT.

"Making Strange" Sean O'Mara

My ideas about how to introduce personality into the commercial design model were turned upside down when studying semiotics, the theory of signs. I found context, more than anything else, defines meaning and interpretation. Using the graphic language of every day forms (found objects/papers/images) in entirely new visual contexts, became a way of making strange familiar messages, and introducing personal obsessions into design work.

Included in this book are some of my designs that play with context, and attempt to use familiar language to carry unfamiliar meanings. Ultimately, I want to provoke a reaction from the viewer who may not anticipate ambiguity.

The discourse of commercial seduction is used, hopefully, to inspire the viewer to look closer and THINK! Graphic design is traditionally about visual relationships connecting ideas, through words and pictures in order to articulate consumer needs. Often, the commercial designer's job is to select and fit material together in the most appropriate, or visually provocative way, to communicate ideas and sell things, rather than to invite interaction. The ultimate aim is to get the design messages across, and to put a personal stamp on the work. It is a task that should invite activity, not passivity, from the audience.

Profile: Sean O'Mara
Born Netherlands 1967. BA Graphic Design (First Class), 1985-1990 Dunlaoghaire College of Art and Design, Dublin. Established Xon Corp Design Studio, Dublin 1990. MA Graphic Design (Distinction), 1991-1993 Central St. Martins College of Art and Design, London. Senior Designer for Imagination Ltd., London 1993-1995. Currently a Senior Designer/Manager for The Body Shop International, London.

"Design as Input" Makoto Orisaki

I guess that limitations on the use of color mostly arise from low budgets. In practice I try to prevent this being a limitation on creativity by moving beyond design as pattern and color, to use unlikely materials and processes such as perforating or embossing that don't involve printing. Working this way, everything hangs on getting hold of materials, finding the right techniques, developing an understanding with technical people working in different fields, and keeping on top of costs — all outside the usual orbit of graphic design, but essential for my work. The result is that I can try out new ideas, keeping within a tight budget, and interact with people designers never usually come across.

In recent years I have been working with industrial grade paper such as cardboard, partly out of a desire to test the Japanese sensitivity to the quality and value of paper. Multimedia is currently all the rage, but it can't convey the feel and quality of paper, and here, I think, lies paper's *forte* as a medium. Paper used in Japan for printing is often a bland, standardized quality, dictated by its perceived suitability. I would like to see greater use of different types of paper, including recycled paper, that have more character. Getting involved myself in the development and production of new materials and techniques, I am finding direct mail design an area where I can experiment with these ideas most effectively.

I'm now working on design that uses no color at all because of its advantages in ease of production and subsequent recycling, and because of its artistic potential.

Profile: Makoto Orisaki
Born 1965. "I have no interest in design as self expression. I'm just concerned to minimize what I call 'human error': choices or actions that have some negative impact. Because the act of giving something form and exposing it to society can exert a certain influence on people's values, lifestyles or cultural perceptions, I feel a sense of responsibility. I believe that designing means using one's insights and producing the best possible answer in every respect — one that's functionally effective, people-friendly, environment-friendly, artistic, humorous.....What you then create transcends the individual designer in its significance."

Einleitung

Als Vorwort zu dieser Sammlung präsentieren wir Ihnen die Kommentare von sechs Designern über das Thema "Design mit ein oder zwei Farben". Sie alle teilen die Ansicht, daß eine Beschränkung hinsichtlich des Gebrauchs von Farbe nicht als Hindernis anzusehen ist, sondern als eine Gelegenheit mit reichem Potential an Gestaltungsmöglichkeiten.

"zwei > vier" cyan

cyan arbeitet ausschließlich im kulturellen bereich. in diesen low- und now-budget-projekten erübrigt sich meist die frage nach aufwendiger reprotechnik, lithografie und vierfarbdruck. daher versuchen wir, die möglichkeiten des ein- und zweifarbdruckes auszuschöpfen und mit diesen zu experimentieren. unabhängig davon ist es für uns auch ästhetisch interessant, mit diesen reduzierten mitteln zu arbeiten. auch der ökologische aspekt ist sehr wichtig. auf die einsparung von filmmaterial, druckplatten, chemie etc. und entsprechende papierauswahl legen wir großen wert..... die reizüberflutung mit << perfekt >> reproduzierter und gedruckter << wirklichkeit >> hat sich unserer meinung nach verbraucht. hight-tech-abbildungsqualität für die angestellten einer versicherungsgesellschaft in einem glänzenden werbeprospekt oder die illustrationen zu einem << heile-welt-verheißenden-bausparangebot >> einer großen bank etc. haben die technischen und ästhetischen möglichkeiten zu sehr strapaziert. davon ausgehend suchen wir nach lösungen, die inhaltlich, haptisch und ästhetisch eine einheit bilden und sich nicht nach einmaligem, kurzem betrachten abnutzen oder auflösen. dazu suchen wir materialien, die weitgehend unnötige chemie ausschließen. die naturpapiere erfordern eine andere bildbearbeitung, da farben anders stehen und wirken. bei der auftragserteilung besprechen wir dies alles mit den auftraggebern, die sich teilweise nur schwer überzeugen lassen. oft wollen sie trotz knappem geld doch etwas buntes und glänzendes. obwohl wir viel erfahrung im mischen und übereinanderdrucken von zwei farben auf naturpapier haben, bleibt es ein spannendes experiment und die farben werden erst an der druckmaschine endgültig abgestimmt.

studio-profil: cyan
"die konzeptionellen überlegungen beschreibt cyan selbst als traditionsbezug auf die gestalterische avantgarde der zwanziger und frühen dreißiger jahre. als vorschlag für eine visuelle kultur, in der die erkenntnis- und elebnisfähigkeit des einzelnen eine entwicklungschance haben. [.....] deshalb die sympathie für die fotografie, der souveräne umgang mit montage- und überblendungstechniken, daher auch die fähigkeit, die alte bodoni in einem neuen ausdrucksumfeld aufzuschließen, kulturelle widersprüche in ästhetische spannungen zu verwandeln, text, bild und papier zu einem ganzen zu verschmelzen, das sich der fast-food-logik im betrachten widersetzt." dr. j. petruschat in novum 2/94

"Die Botschaft des Kunden durch Farbe kommunizieren"
Stoere Binken Design

Wir arbeiten gerne öfters mit nur einer oder zwei Farben. Dies gibt dem Artwork eine ästhetische Reinheit und Abstraktion, die beim Vierfarbdruck oft verlorengeht. Natürlich ist ein weiterer, nicht weniger wichtiger Aspekt der Ein- und Zweifarb-Arbeiten, daß sie dem Kunden eine Menge Geld sparen. Viele Male ist dies der Hauptgrund dafür, mit limitierten Farben zu arbeiten.

Mit zwei Farben zu gestalten, vermittelt totale Kontrolle über die Intensität der Farben. Die Fusion von zwei Farben produziert weitere Farben, die wiederum in unzählige Nuancen variiert werden können. Auf diese Weise kann man auch mit Überlagerungen arbeiten, die weniger zweidimensional wirken, Atmosphäre schaffen und die Emotionen des Betrachters stimulieren.

Auf diese Weise mit Farbe zu experimentieren, bringt uns näher zu dem, was gutes Design ausmacht: die Botschaft auf eine direkte, ehrliche und profunde Weise zu kommunizieren. Gutes Design heißt nicht, schöne Dinge zu machen, sondern eine graphische Sprache zu schaffen, die den Intentionen des Kunden dient.

Unglücklicherweise hat die Multimedia-Explosion der letzten Zeit den Rahmen für auffallende, rapide wechselnde Vierfarb-Bilder geschaffen, die kaum dafür genutzt werden, die Aufmerksamkeit des Betrachters zu bekommen. Zu oft wird die Botschaft in diesem Prozeß erstickt.

Studio-Profil: Stoere Binken Design
Wir sind ein ziemlich junges Graphik-Design Studio, beheimatet im holländischen Maastricht. Unser Studio besteht aus zwei guten Freunden. Wir begannen sofort nach dem Studium an der Hochschule der Künste in Maastricht. Wir operieren (inter)national und haben eine Vielzahl von Klienten. Unsere Arbeiten reichen von Firmenerscheinungsbildern zu CD-Covers, Zeitschriften, Flugblättern u.a. Wir haben unsere eigenen Ansichten über Design — und darum werden wir von unseren Kunden ausgewählt.

"Das Objekt von zwei Farben"
Darin Beaman

Über 60 Prozent aller Projekte am Art Center sind in einer oder zwei Farben. Das liegt an den begrenzten Mitteln im akademischen Umfeld. Manch einer denkt, daß diese Beschränkungen auch das Design limitieren. Wir sehen jedoch jede einzelne Drucksache als eine Gelegenheit, unsere visuellen Ausdrucksmöglichkeiten zu entwickeln und auszuweiten.

Ein gutes Beispiel dafür ist der in diesem Buch gezeigte Ausstellungskatalog für *Objects* (pg.132). Die Auflage und das Budget waren klein, das Thema jedoch hochinteressant; es schien eine einzigartige Lösung zu verlangen. Die Form des Katalogs betont die Absicht, dieses Buches als Objekt zu betrachten. Wir zeigten die Fäden der Bindung und das Bindeleinen, um deren Dinglichkeit als Teil des Buch-Produktionsprozesses zu betonen. Wir nahmen dem Katalog seinen Umschlagdeckel und benutzen Deckpapier für die Textseiten, alles der Strategie folgend, das Buch zu "entmaterialisieren". Diese Elemente wurden kombiniert, um eine subtile Verwirrung der Kategorien Buch und Objekt zu schaffen.

Wir sind besonders bei kleineren Projekten dazu verpflichtet, Risiken zu übernehmen und unkonventionelle Optionen für Konzeption und Produktion auszuprobieren. Wir sind allerdings darauf eingeschworen, auf jedes Detail zu achten, wissen wir doch nie, wohin uns das Projekt führt oder welches neue Denken es inspirieren mag.

Studio-Profil: Design Büro für Art Center College of Design
1986 vom Präsidenten David R. Brown gegründet, ist das Art Center Design Büro verantwortlich für alle Drucksachen des Colleges, Stuart Frolick, Vizepräsident und Creative Director steht dem Büro seit 1987 vor. Der Designer Darin Beaman kam 1991 zum Art Center. Die hier gezelgten Arbeiten wurden über eine Fünf-Jahres-Periode von zwei Art Directoren, fünf Designern und einer kleinen Produktionsmannschaft fertiggestellt.

"Verrücktes tun"   Sean O'Mara

Meine Ideen darüber, wie man Persönlichkeit in das Modell der kommerziellen Gestaltung bringt, wurden auf den Kopf gestellt, als ich Semiotik, die Theorie der Zeichen, studierte. Ich fand, daß der Kontext mehr als alles andere Bedeutung und Interpretation definiert. Durch den Gebrauch der graphischen Sprache der Alltagsformen (Fundsachen/Papiere/ Bilder) in vollkommen neuem visuellen Kontext ergab sich ein Weg, verrückte, vertraute Botschaften zu machen — und persönliche Besessenheit in die Gestaltungsarbeit einzubringen.

In diesem Buch gibt es einige meiner Designs, die mit Kontext spielen und versuchen, durch den Gebrauch einer vertrauten Sprache unvertraute Bedeutungen zu transportieren. Letztendlich will ich den Betrachter, der diese Mehrdeutigkeit nicht erwartet haben mag, zu einer Reaktion provozieren.

Der Diskurs der kommerziellen Sättigung wird benutzt, so hoffe ich, um die Betrachter anzuregen, genauer hinzuschauen und zu DENKEN. Beim Graphik-Design geht es traditionell um visuelle Beziehungen, um die Verbindung von Worten und Bildern, darum die Bedürfnisse der Kunden zu artikulieren. Oft ist es die Aufgabe des Graphik-Designers, Material auszuwählen und zusammenzufügen, auf die ansprechendste Art oder auf visuell provozierende Weise. Damit sollen Ideen kommuniziert und Dinge verkauft werden, mehr als um zu Interaktion einzuladen. Das letztendliche Ziel ist es, die Design-Botschaft hinüberzubringen und der Arbeit einen persönlichen Stempel aufzudrücken. Es ist eine Aufgabe, die das Publikum zu Aktivität einladen sollte, nicht zur Passivität.

Profil: Sean O'Mara
Geboren in Holland 1967. Ausbildung in Graphik-Design am Dunlaoghaire College of Art and Design, Dublin, 1985-1990. Gründung des Xon Corp Design Studio, Dublin, 1990. Weiterbildung im Graphik-Design am Central St. Martins College of Art and Design, London, 1991-1993. Leitender Designer bei Imagination Ltd., London, 1993-1995. Heute Leitender Designer für The Body Shop International, London.

"Design als Input"   Makoto Orisaki

Vermutlich kommen Beschränkungen im Gebrauch von Farben durch Budgetrestriktionen. Ich versuche, dies nicht zu einer Limitierung der Kreativität werden zu lassen. Design sehe ich nicht nur als Textur und Farbe, ich verwende auch besondere Materialien und außergewöhnliche Bearbeitungsverfahren wie Perforation, Stanzung und Prägung. Um die Kosten niedrig zu halten, hängt bei dieser Arbeitsweise alles davon ab, das richtige Material und die richtigen Techniken zu finden. Das geht oft über den üblichen Horizont des Graphik-Design hinaus, aber ohne dem geht es für mich nicht. Ich kann so neue Ideen ausprobieren und auch mit Leuten interagieren, mit denen ich sonst kaum in Kontakt käme.

In den letzten Jahren arbeite ich mit Industriepapieren wie z. B. solches für Verpackungen, auch um die Sensitivität der Japaner hinsichtlich Qualität und Wert von Papier zu testen. Multimedia ist heute das Schlagwort. Damit kann man aber nicht das Gefühl von Papier vermitteln - und darin liegt ja gerade die Stärke des Papiers als Medium. Meist wird in Japan standardisiertes Druckpapier verwandt, bestimmt durch seine jeweilige Eignung für das Druckverfahren. Ich selbst würde gerne intensiveren Gebrauch verschiedener Papiertypen sehen, einschließlich dem von Recyclingpapier. Diese Papiere sind charaktervoller. Am effektivsten kann ich bei Direct Mailings auf die Entwicklung und die Produktion neuer Materialien einwirken.

Kürzlich habe ich mit Designs begonnen, die überhaupt keine Farbe mehr brauchen. Das vereinfacht die Produktion und das Recycling - und eröffnet ein neues künstlerisches Potential.

Profil: Makoto Orisaki
Geboren 1965 "Ich habe überhaupt kein Interesse an Design als Mittel der Selbstdarstellung. Ich versuche, das was ich 'menschlichen Fehler' nenne, zu minimieren: Entscheidungen oder Aktionen mit negativem Einfluß. Weil der Formgebungsakt und die Konfrontationen der Gesellschaft mit der Arbeit einen Einfluß auf die Werte der Leute, ihren Lebensstil oder ihre kulturelle Aufnahme ausübt, habe ich ein Gefühl der Verantwortlichkeit. Für mich ist das Gestalten der Gebrauch von Einsichten und die Darstellung der bestmöglichen, positiven Antwort in jeder Hinsicht - eine, die hinsichtlich ihrer Funktion effektiv ist, menschenfreundlich, umweltfreundlich, künstlerisch, humorvoll und so weiter. Was man dann schafft, transzendiert den individuellen Designer in seiner Bedeutung."

"Erinnerungen an Farbe"
Jean-Benoît Lévy

Was ist Ihre Lieblingsfarbe, Sie, der Sie diesen Text lesen? Bei mir persönlich wechselt sie, je nach Stimmung und manchmal auch nach Jahreszeit.

Bei Nacht, bei Tag und bei den verschiedenen Lichtarten ist Farbe ständig in Konfrontation mit ihrer Umgebung. Genau wie Photographie und Typographie ist die Auswahl der Farben essentiell. Farben existieren durch die Gefühle, die sie erzeugen. Sobald diese determiniert sind, ist die Frage nicht mehr "Wie viele Farben?" sondern "Welche Farben?"

Im Falle der Serie von Theaterplakaten, die ich für Basel schuf, las ich erst die Stücke bevor ich anfing, so daß mein Design mit dem aufgeführten Stück korrespondieren konnte. Ich fand, daß Autoren ihre Texte oft damit beginnen, spezifische Plätze (eine Stadt, ein Wald), eine Tageszeit (Morgen, Abend) oder eine Umgebung (im Haus, im Freien) vorzustellen, die dann auf eine oder mehrere Farben anspielen.

Ich erlaube mir auch, mich durch das, was ich um mich herum sehe, beeinflussen zu lassen: Mode, andere Graphik-Designs, innovative Flyer, verwobene Kombinationen in der Natur und sogar durch Zufälligkeiten, wie beim Auswaschen meiner Pinsel. Bewußt über die Wichtigkeit solcher "visuellen Momente", versuche ich sie in meinem "Farbgedächtnis" zu halten.

Nachdem eine künstlerische Richtung eingeschlagen ist, entwickeln sich Farben kontinuierlich weiter, sogar bis hin zur Produktion. Es ist beim Drucker an der Druckmaschine, wo die letzten Entscheidungen über Ton, Transparenz, Tiefe und Sättigung gefällt werden. Und später, wenn ich das Plakat in den Strassen hängen sehe, kann ich letztendlich sehen, ob die Farbentscheidungen die richtigen waren.

Welche Farben werden Sie heute tragen? Wählen Sie sie gut, denn sie werden auch ein Spiegel Ihrer Persönlichkeit sein !

Profil: Jean-Benoît Lévy
Geboren 1959. 1978-1983 Vorkurs und anschliessend die Grafikfachklasse der Schule für Gestaltung in Basel. 1983-1986 Grafiker für die Schweizer Mustermesse. Sommer 1987 Presse-Grafiker in Lausanne für zwei Magazine. 1987 ein halbes Jahr in San-Francisco, als Freelancer. Zurück in Basel eröffnete er im Sommer 1988 sein eigenes Atelier "And, Trafic Grafic". 1991-1996 unterrichtete er einmal wöchentlich am "Art Center College of Design Europe". 1993-1994 war er ebenso in der Schule für Gestaltung in Basel. Im Winter 1995-1996 für Wintersession in der "RISD" (Rhode Island School of Design) in Providence, USA, als Gastdozent tätig. Seine Tätigkeit umfasst das ganze Spektrum zwischen Grafik und Werbung. Er hat gerade eine Briefmarke für die Schweizer PTT realisiert.

editorial notes

Credit Format クレジットフォーマット

Creative Staff 制作スタッフ
- CD: Creative director
- AD: Art director
- D: Designer
- P: Photographer
- I: Illustrator
- CW: Copywriter
- PD: Producer
- DF: Design firm
- A: Agency
- CL: Client

Country from which submitted 国名
Year of completion 制作年

カラーサンプルについて

本書は4色のプロセスカラーで印刷されています。参考資料として各クレジットの端にカラーサンプルを掲載しましたが、実際の作品の色とは多少異なるものもあることをあらかじめご了承ください。(カラーサンプルは各作品提供者からの情報をもとにしていますが、情報が不足している一部作品については小社で色を判断しました。)
また蛍光色・メタリックカラーについては下記記号で表記しました。
F = (Fluorescent ink)　蛍光色
M = (Metallic ink)　　メタリックカラー

Color Samples

This book has been printed using the standard 4-color printing process. The credit details include color samples given for reference purposes, which may vary slightly from the actual color of the artwork due to the printing process.

The color samples are based on information received from our contributors. In a small number of cases where the information was insufficient, the editors have made their own judgement.

Abbreviations are used to indicate special inks as follows:
F = fluorescent ink
M = metallic ink

提供者の意向により、クレジットデータの一部に掲載していないものがあります。

Please note that some credit data has been omitted at the request of the submittor.

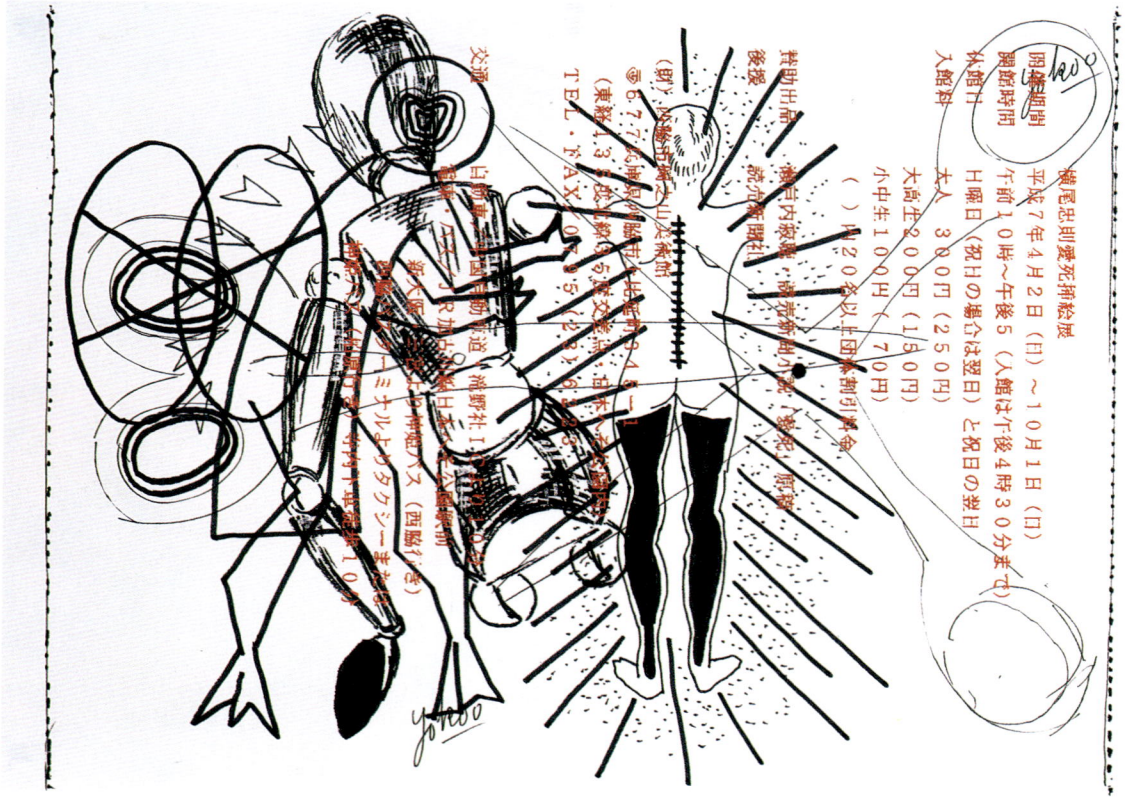

1. D: Daniela Haufe / Detlef Fiedler DF: Cyan CL: Bauhaus Dessau Germany 1995

2. AD, D, I: Tadanori Yokoo CL: Okanoyama Museum of Art Japan 1995

D: Daniela Haufe / Detlef Fiedler DF: Cyan CL: Form + Zweck Germany 1994

AD: U-cef Hanjani D: Martin Venezky P: Robert Olding CW: Bob Rickert A: J. Walter Thompson San Francisco
CL: San Francisco AIDS Foundation - Needle Exchange USA 1996

POSTERS

1. CD, D: Seán O'Mara P: Teelesh Bisnauthsing DF, CL: Xon Corp   UK   1993

2. CD, D, P: Seán O'Mara DF: Xon Corp CL: Turning Point   UK   1991

1. AD, D: Osamu Fukushima CL: Yamanote Jijohsha Japan 1996
2. AD, D: Osamu Fukushima CL: Yamanote Jijohsha Japan 1996

POSTERS

AD, D, I: Gugi Akiyama CL: Shinchosha Japan 1994

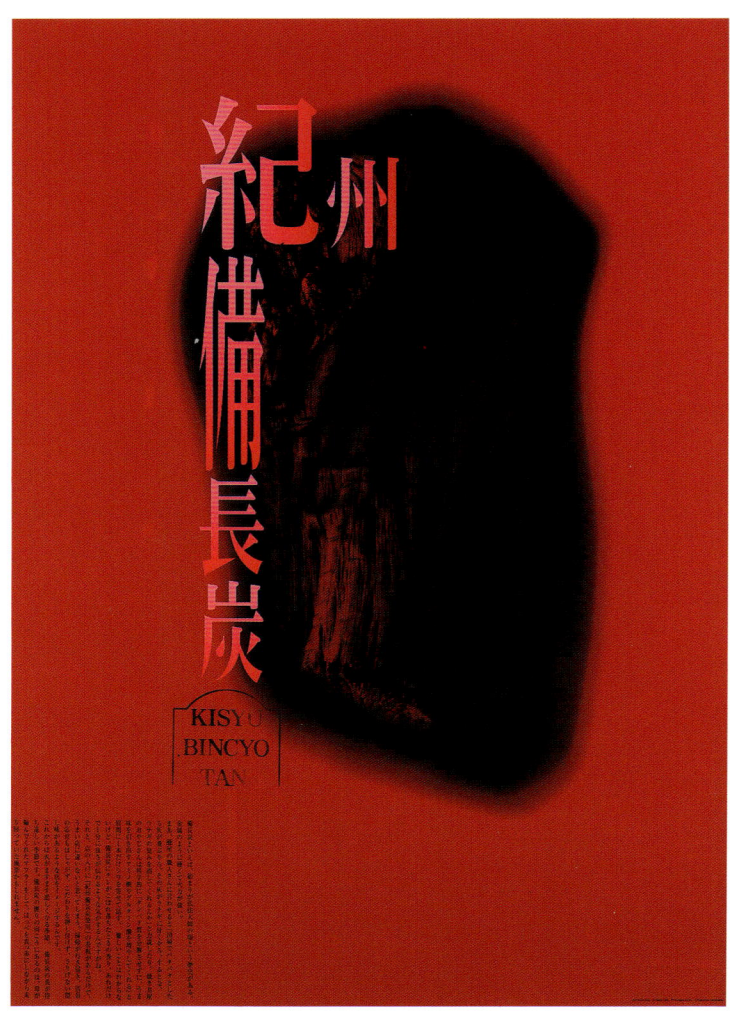

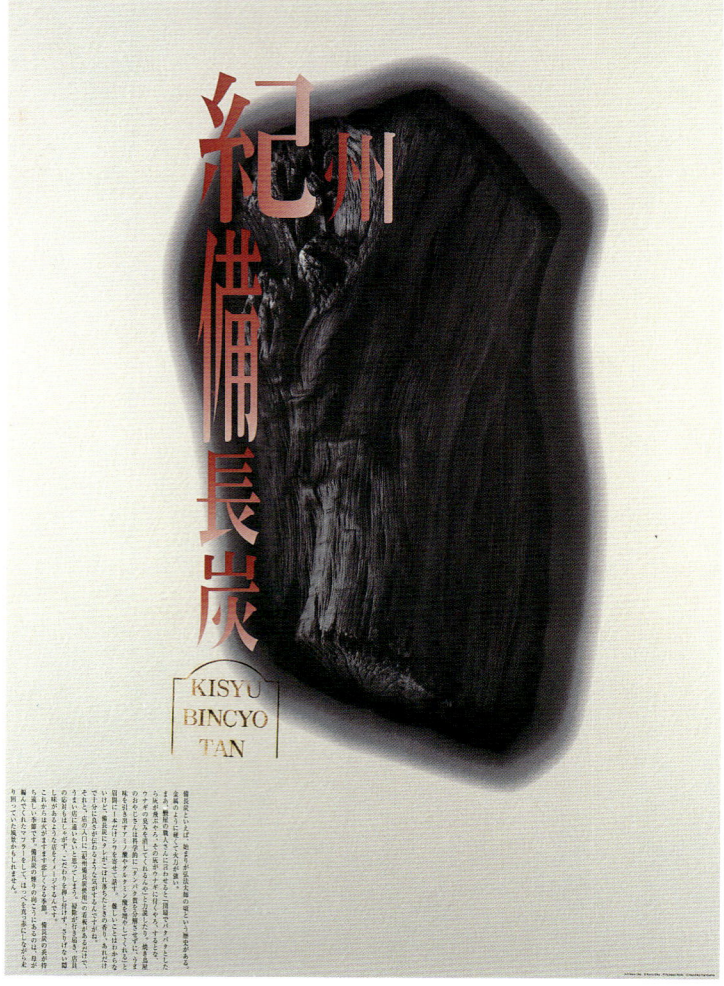

CD, AD, D: Kisei Oka P: Tsukasa Horie CW: Kazuhiko Kamiyama CL: Creative Studio Beans   Japan 1995
*Heat-stamped 焼き印

AD: Yukio Ikoma D: Yumiko Kawasaki P: Yasuto Okumura CL: JAGDA Japan 1995

POSTERS

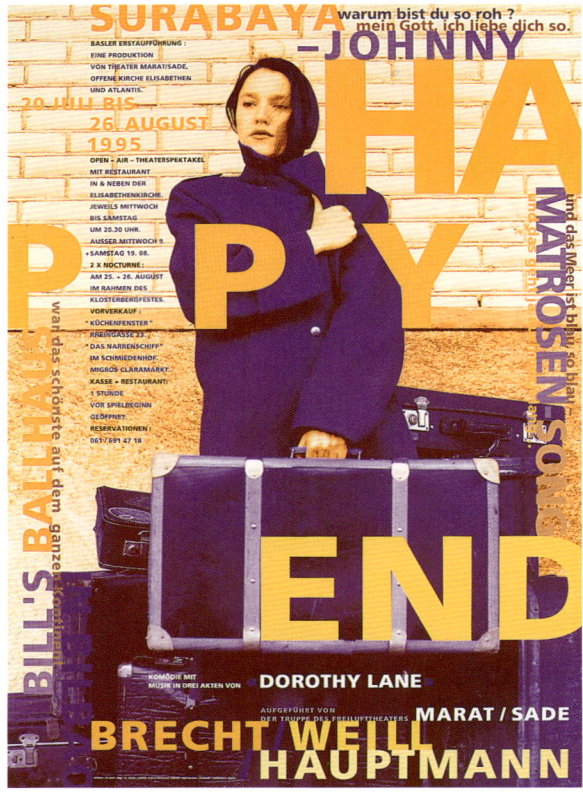

1, 2, 4 CD, AD, D: Jean-Benoît Lévy P: Stefan Meichtry Silkscreen: Albin Uldry DF: AND (Trafic Grafic)
CL: Theater Marat - Sade Switzerland 1. 1995 / 2. 1993 / 4. 1992

3 CD, AD, D: Jean-Benoît Lévy P: Martin Klotz Silkscreen: Albin Uldry DF: AND (Trafic Grafic) CL: Theater Marat - Sade Switzerland 1996

1. AD, D: Yusaku Tomoeda CL: JAGDA Japan 1993
2. AD, D: Yusaku Tomoeda CL: JAGDA Japan 1995

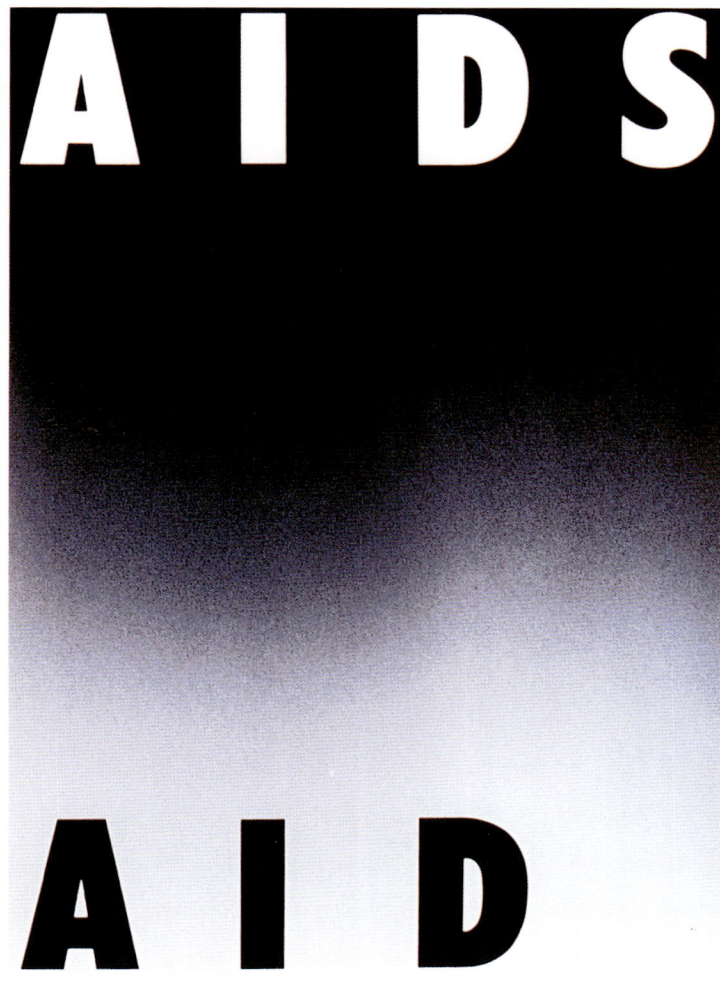

1. AD, D: Koichi Sato CL: Tokyo Art Directors Club Japan 1993

2. AD, D: Koichi Sato CL: Tokyo Art Directors Club Japan 1993

POSTERS

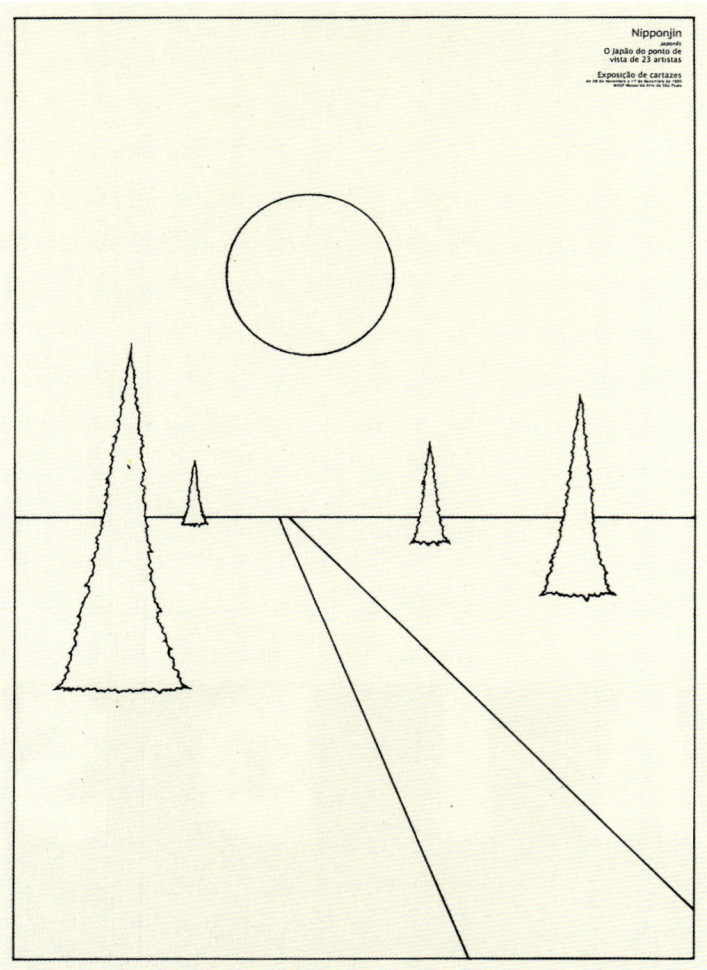
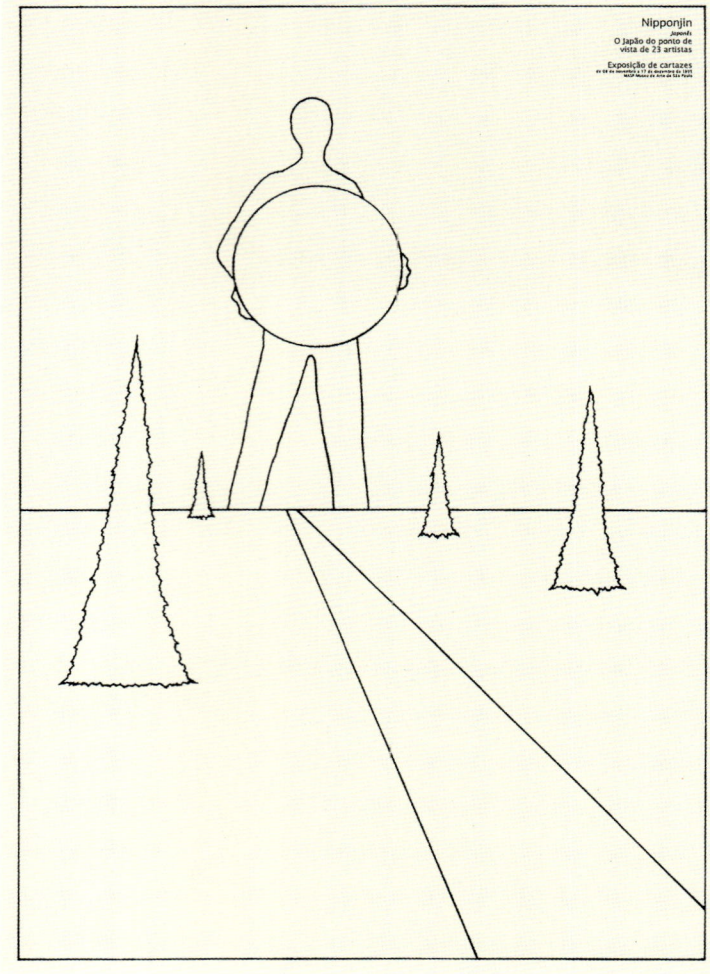

AD, I: Keiji Ito Coordinator: Takako Terunuma DF: Lop Lop Design CL: MASP Japan 1996

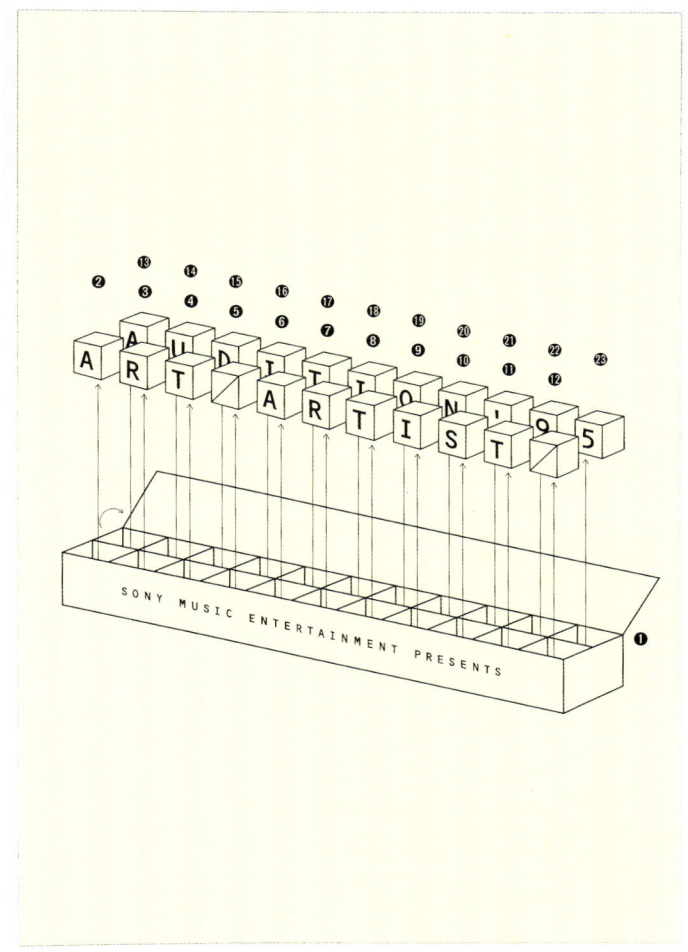

1. AD, D: Norio Nakamura CL: Tempozan Contemporary Museum Japan 1996
*Varnish

2. AD: Norio Nakamura D: Hiromi Watanabe CL: Sony Music Entertainment (Japan) Inc. Japan 1995
*Varnish

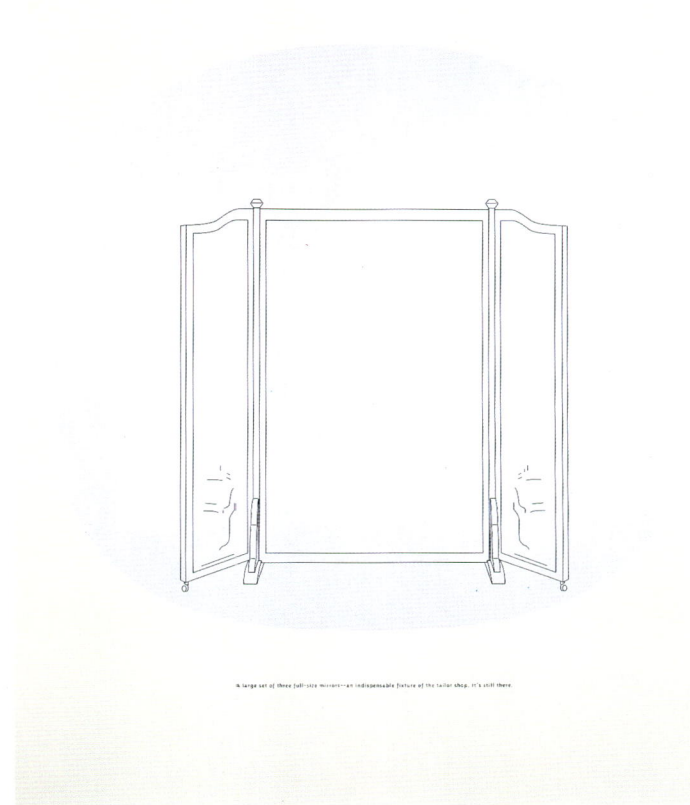

1, 2 **AD, D, I:** Katsunori Aoki   Japan   1992

3, 4 **AD, D, I:** Katsunori Aoki   Japan   1995

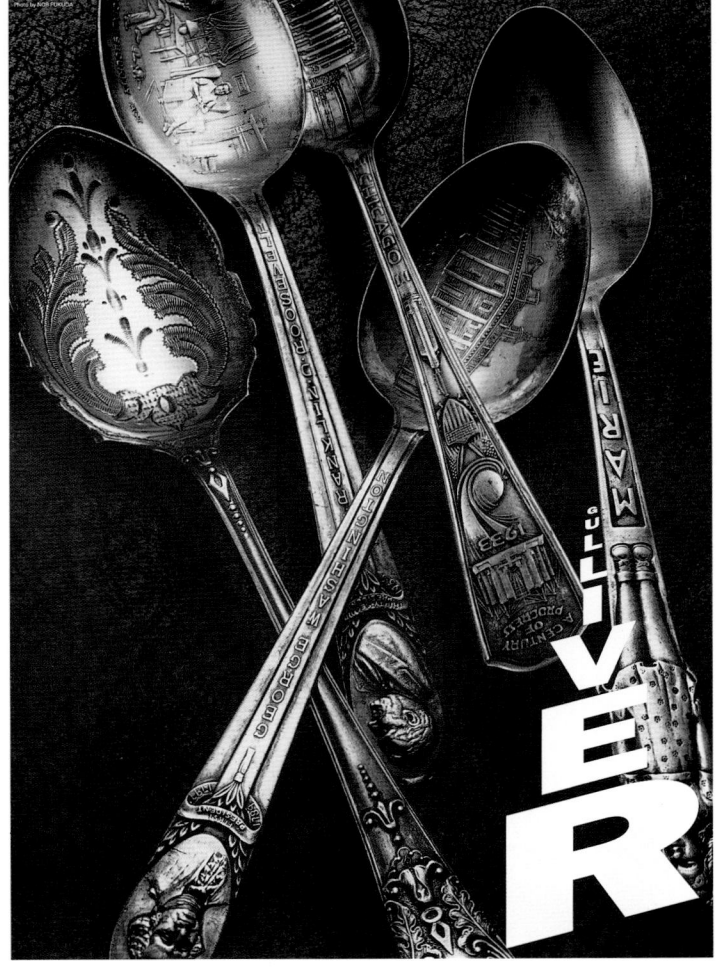

1. AD, D: Akio Okumura DF: Packaging Create Inc. CL: New Oji Paper Co., Ltd. Japan 1996

2. AD: Akio Okumura D: Mitsuo Ueno P: Nob Fukuda DF: Packaging Create Inc. CL: New Oji Paper Co., Ltd. Japan 1996

D: Daniela Haufe / Detlef Fiedler DF: Cyan CL: Bauhaus Dessau Germany 1994-1996

POSTERS

D: Daniela Haufe / Detlef Fiedler DF: Cyan CL: Bauhaus Dessau Germany 1994-1996

POSTERS

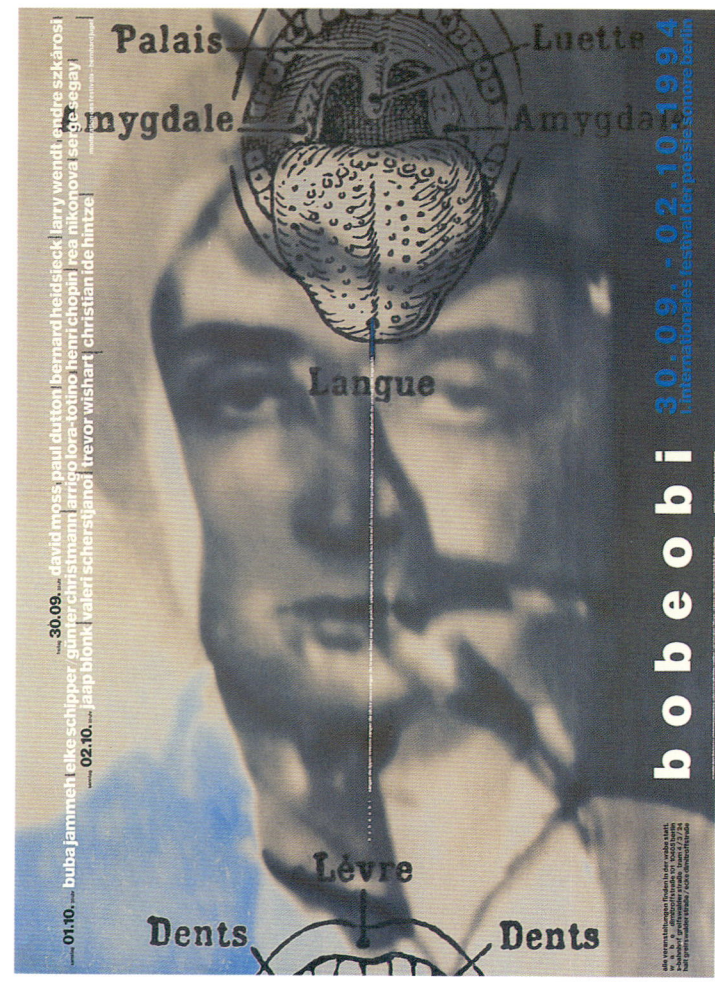

32

1. D: Daniela Haufe / Detlef Fiedler DF: Cyan CL: Kampagne Gegen Wehrdflicht Germany 1991 *Anti-war poster

2. D: Daniela Haufe / Detlef Fiedler DF: Cyan CL: Förderband E. V. Germany 1994

POSTERS

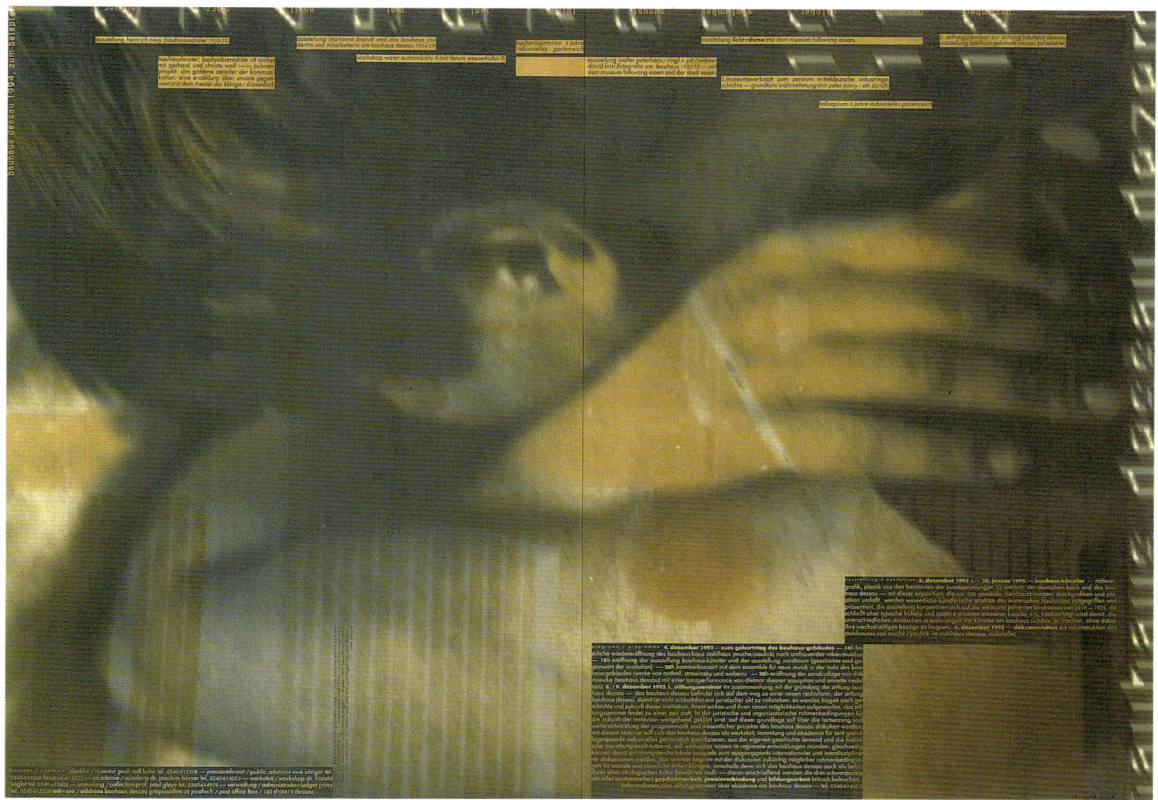

1. D: Daniela Haufe / Detlef Fiedler DF: Cyan CL: Bauhaus Dessau   Germany 1994-1996

2. D, P: Daniela Haufe D: Detlef Fiedler DF: Cyan CL: Kammeroper Berlin Germany 1995

1. CD, P, I: Elliott Peter Earls CL: The Apollo Program USA
2. CD, P, I: Elliott Peter Earls CL: The Apollo Program USA

F **M**   CD, AD, D: Pascal Béjean   P: Denis Majorel   DF, CL: Bleu Élastique   France   1996

1. CD, AD, D: Silvana Mattievich CL: Centro Cultural Banco do Brasil Brazil 1996

2. AD, D: Emanuel Barbosa DF: Emanuel Barbosa Design CL: Câmara Municipal do Porto Portugal 1995

1. CD, AD, D, I: Sonia Greteman D: James Strange CL: Connect Care AIDS Program USA 1995

2. CD, AD, D, I: Don Weller DF: The Weller Institute for the Cure of Design, Inc. CL: Park City Performances USA 1994

AD, D: Morisato Tomura P: Muga Miyahara I, Calligrapher: Aki Hamiru Model: Noriko Iwabuchi CD: Lucas Badtke - Berkow
DF: Friendships Tokyo CL: Tokion Japan 1996

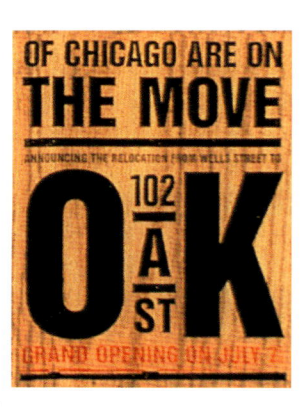

1. CD, AD, D: Carlos Segura DF: Segura Inc. CL: Elements USA 1996

2. CD, AD, D, I: John Sayles DF: Sayles Graphic Design CL: American Institute of Architects USA 1996

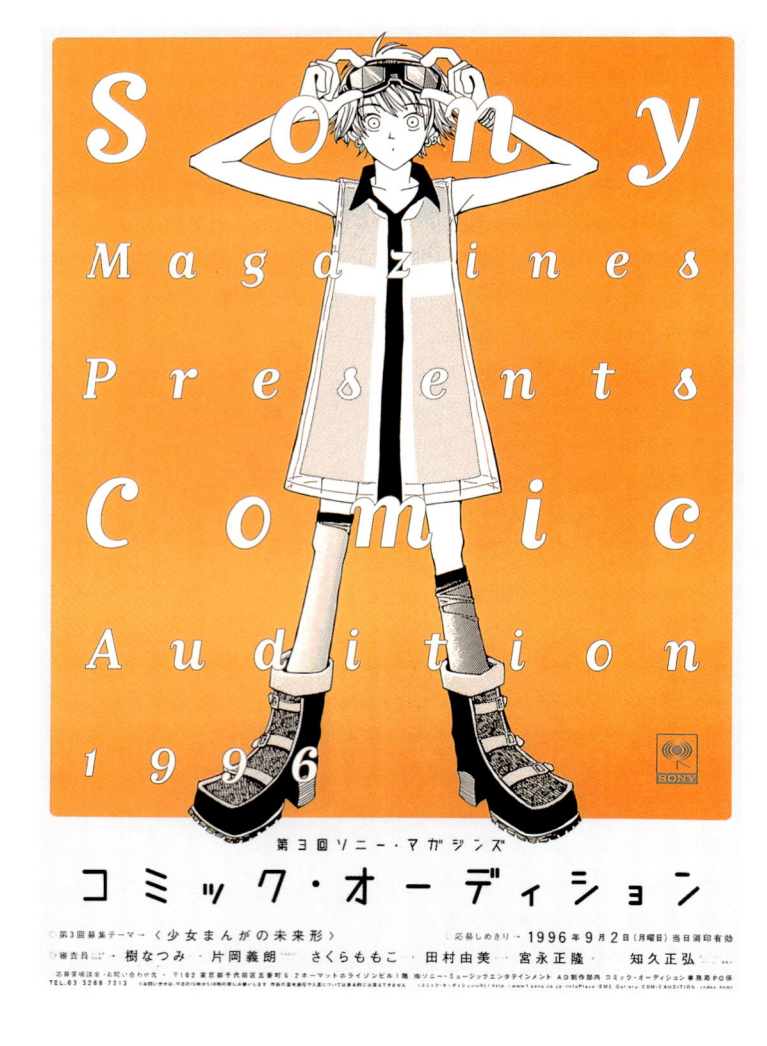

1. CD: Dana Arnett AD: Curt Schreiber D: Ken Fox DF: VSA Partners, Inc. CL: Harley - Davidson USA 1992

2. AD, D: Hiromi Watanabe I: Iruka Ikaruga CL: Sony Music Entertainment (Japan) Inc. / Sony Magazines Japan 1996

1. CD: Masahide Norikuni D: Chieko Maenishi DF: Sankyo Agency Co., Ltd. CL: Sun TV Japan 1995

2. AD: Dana Arnett D: Curt Schreiber DF: VSA Partners CL: Harley Davidson Motor Co. USA 1994

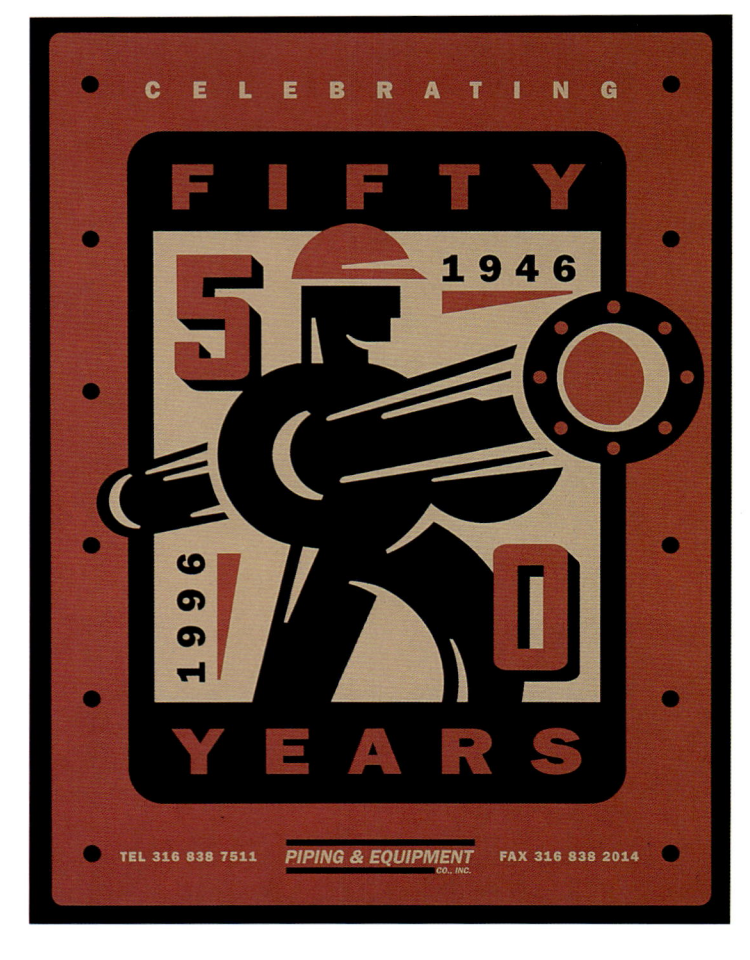

1. CD, AD, D, I: Bjorn Akselsen Computer Art: Pattie Belle Hastings DF: Icehouse Design CL: The Atlanta College of Art USA 1993

2. CD, AD: Sonia Greteman AD, D: James Strange CL: Piping & Equipment USA 1996

POSTERS

1. D, Sculptor: Daniel R. Smith P: Sean Bolan DF: Command Z CL: Fenix   USA   1996

2. CD, AD, D: Michel Bouvet P: Francis Laharrague CL: Maison des Arts, Créteil   France   1992

43

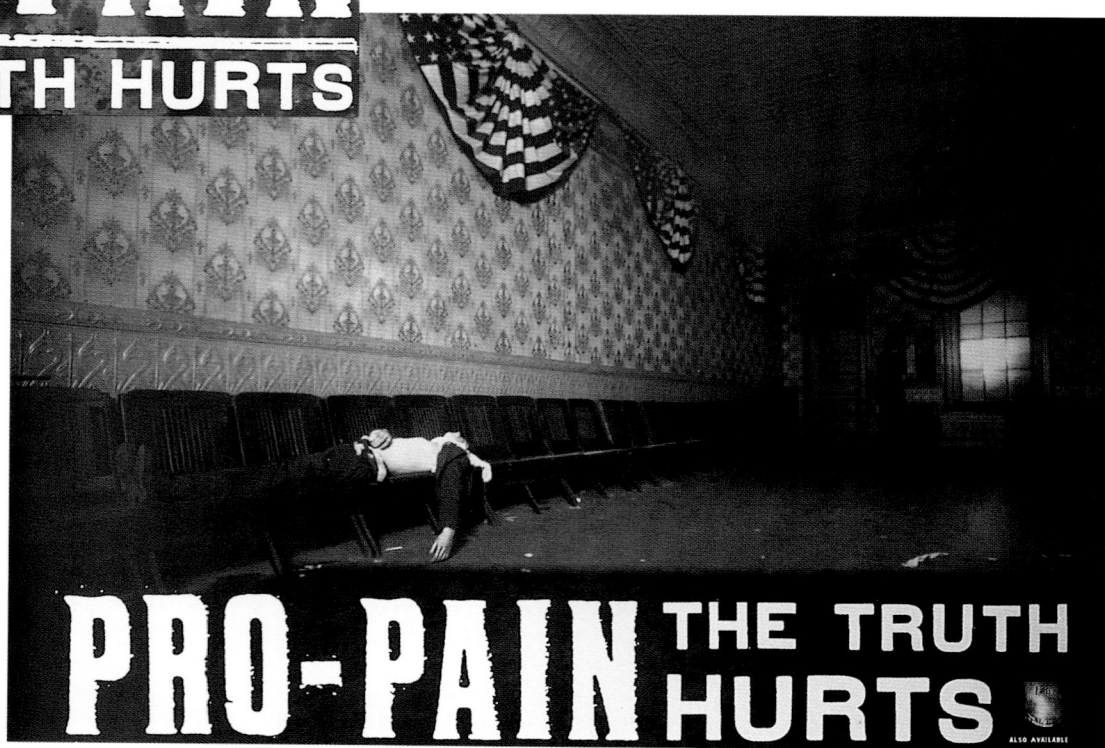

CD, AD: Stefan Sagmeister D: Veronica Oh DF: Sagmeister Inc. CL: Energy Records   USA 1995

POSTERS

1. CD, AD, D, DF: Ralph Schraivogel Printer: Albin Uldry CL: Zurich Film Podium Switzerland 1996

2. CD, AD, D: Stefan Sagmeister P: Timothy Greenfield Sanders DF: Sagmeister Inc. CL: Warner Brothers USA 1996

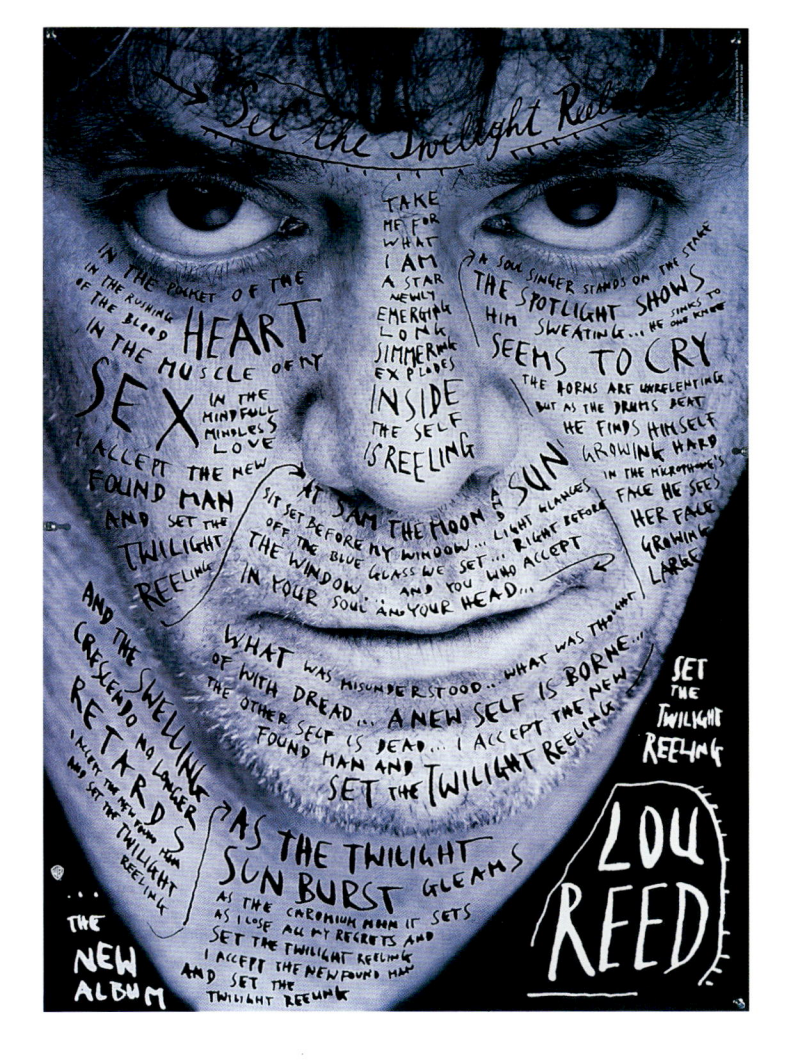

POSTERS

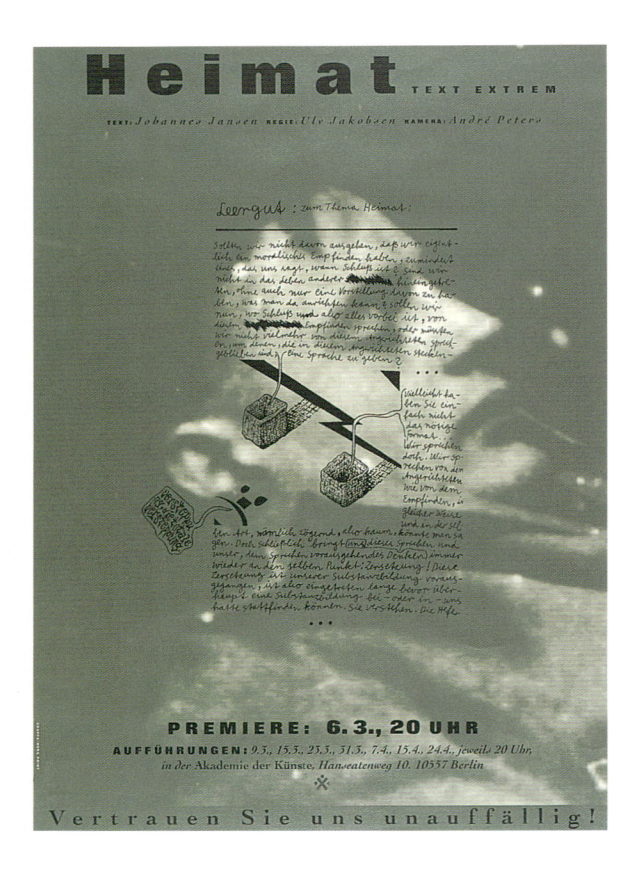

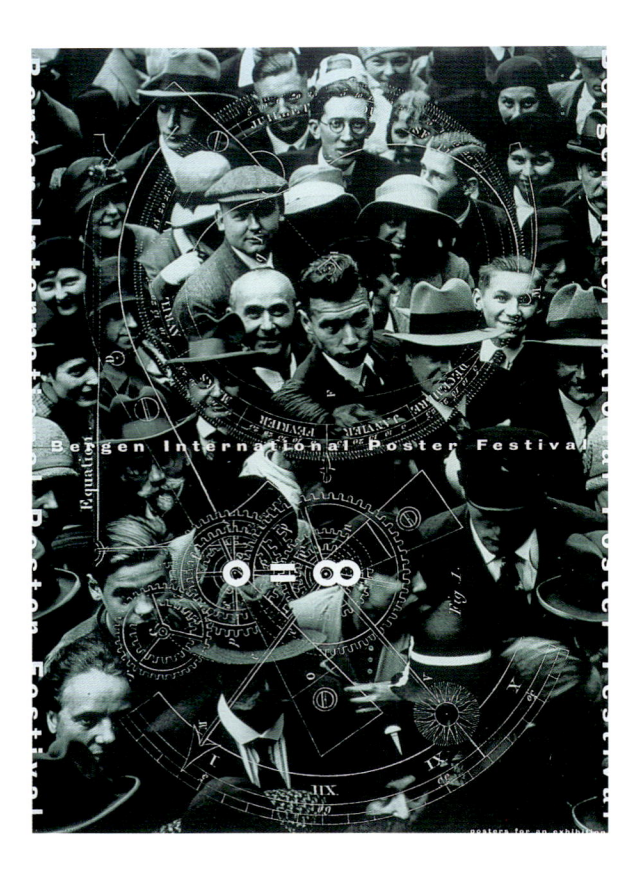

1. CD, AD, D: Ute Zscharnt I: Johanna Jansen CL: Akademie der Künste Germany

2. CD, AD, D: Dieter Feseke P: Xanti Schawinski (Bauhaus) DF: Grappa Design CL: Angon Jonnsen & Bernt Germany 1993

3. CD, AD, D: Dieter Feseke P, CL: Stiftung Bauhaus Dessau DF: Grappa Design Germany 1995

4. CD, AD, D, P, I: Andreas Trogisch / Dieter Feseke CL: Berliner Film Kunsthaus Germany 1992

5. CD, AD, D, P: Heike Grebin / Andreas Trogisch DF: Grappa Design CL: Bergen Poster Festival Germany 1993

6. CD, AD, D, P: Heike Grebin / Andreas Trogisch DF: Grappa Design CL: Filmmuseum Potsdam Germany 1995

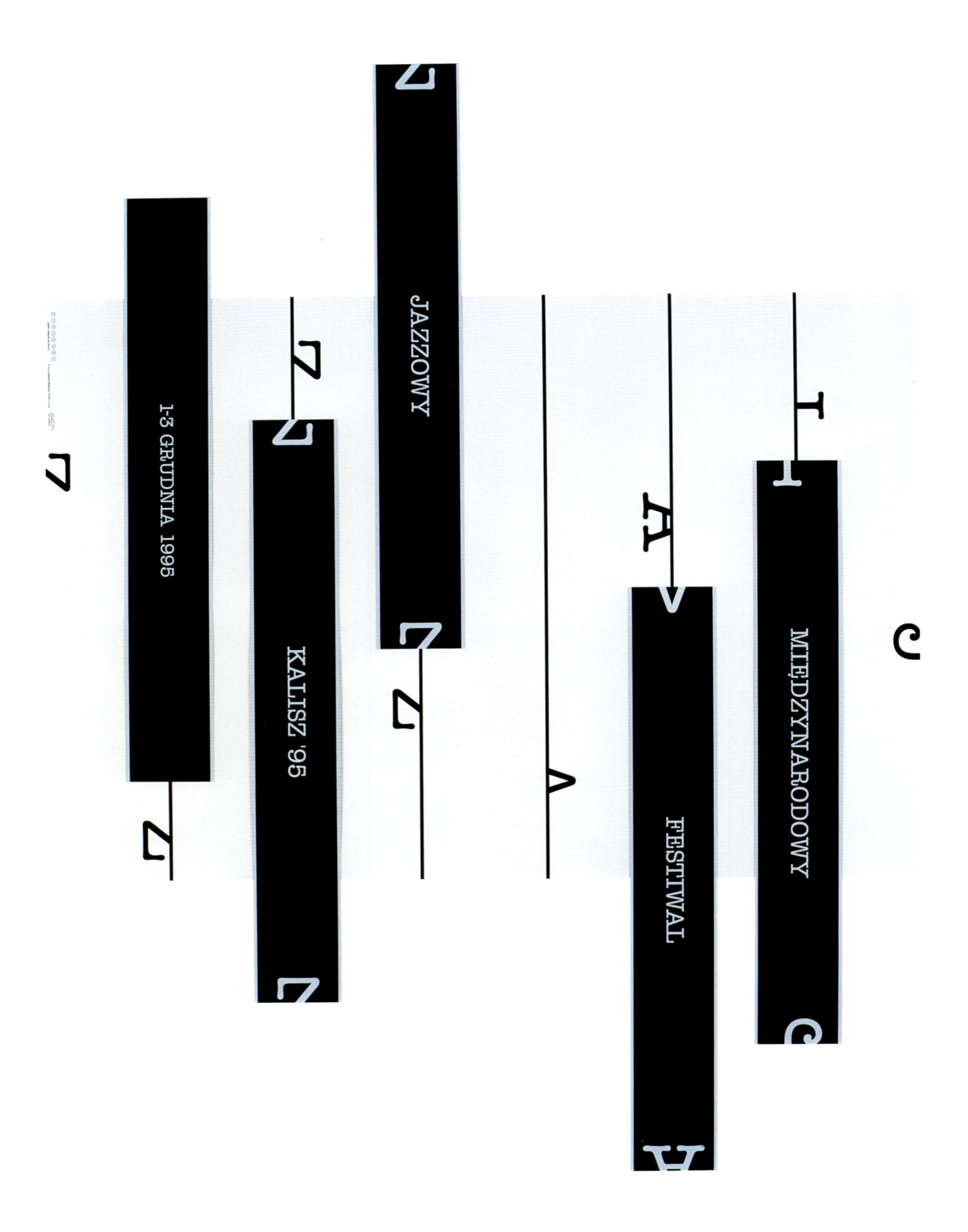

POSTERS

1. CD, AD, D: Tadeusz Piechura DF: Atelier Tadeusz Piechura CL: W. D. K. - Kalisz Poland 1995

2. AD, D: Norio Kudo P: Takahito Sato DF: Magna Inc. Advertising CL: JAGDA Japan 1995

POSTERS

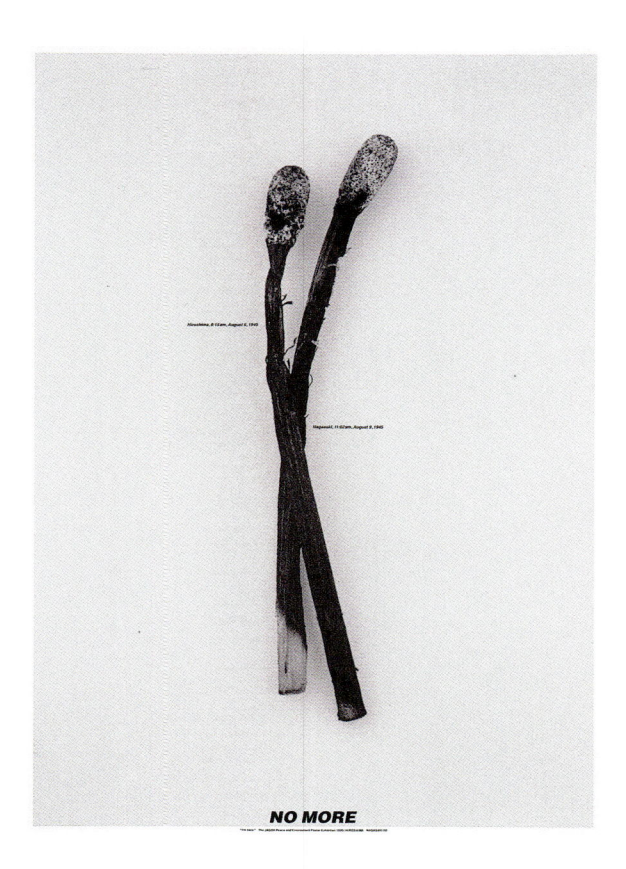

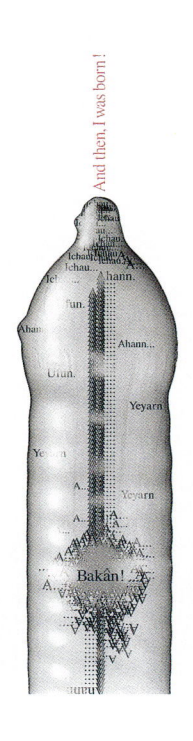

3. AD, D, I: Norio Nakamura CL: Gallery Preview Japan 1995

4. CD: Yoshifumi Shibukawa AD: Keisuke Kimura D: Maki Yanagishima P: Kyoko Harada CL: Toyo Information Systems Co., Ltd. Japan 1996

5. AD: Keisuke Kimura D: Maki Yanagishima P: Naohiro Isshiki CL: Rakuten Design Room Japan 1996

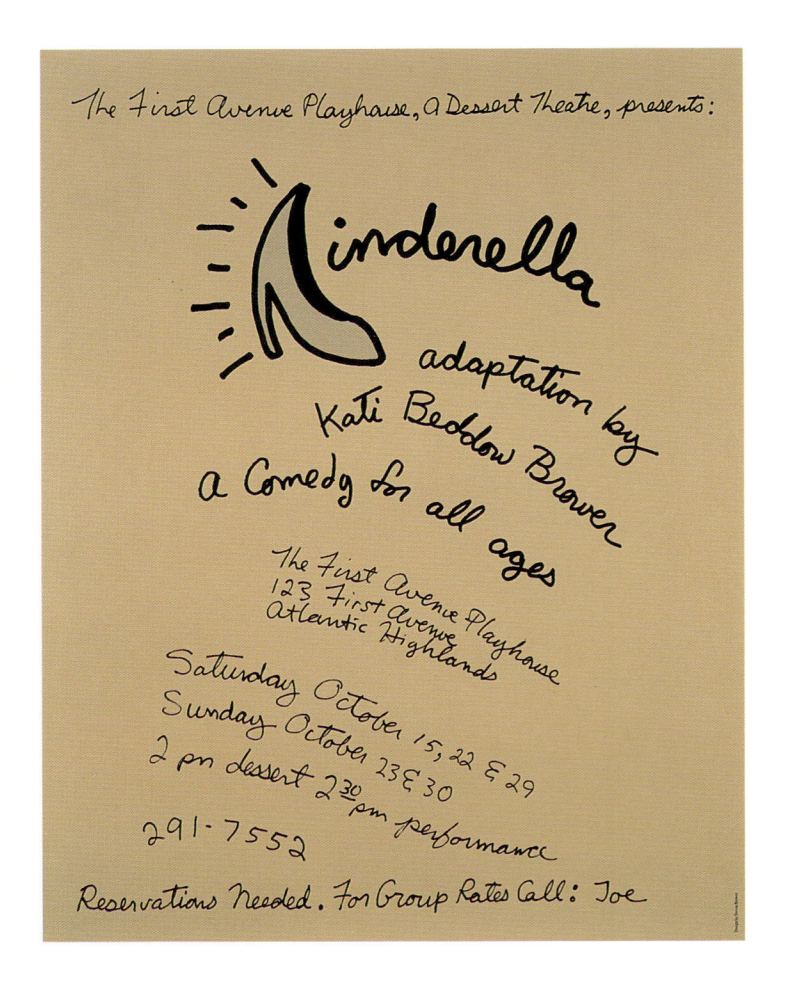

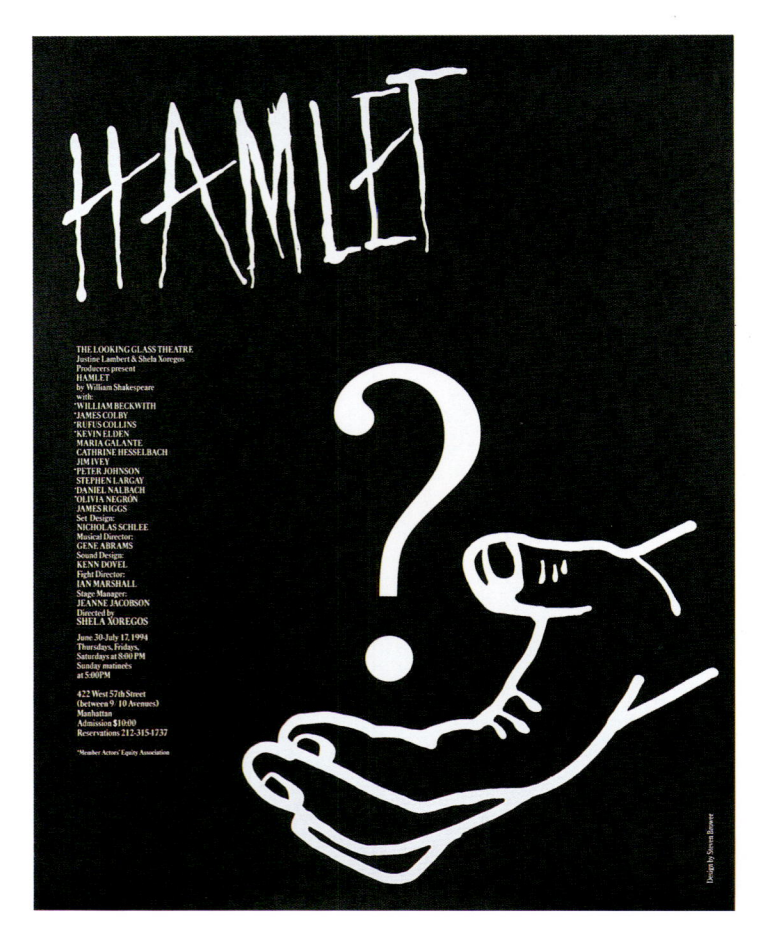

POSTERS

50

1. **AD, D, I:** Steven Brower **DF:** Steven Brower Design **CL:** First Avenue Play House USA 1994
*Varnish

2. **AD, D, I:** Steven Brower **DF:** Steven Brower Design **CL:** The Looking Glass Theatre USA 1994

POSTERS

1. D: Kees Wagenaars P: M. Verhoeven DF: Case CL: Teater '77 Netherlands 1995

2. D: Kess Wagenaars DF: Case CL: Teater '77 Netherlands 1994

3. D: Kees Wagenaars I: Sieb DF: Case CL: Zaal 16 Netherlands 1996

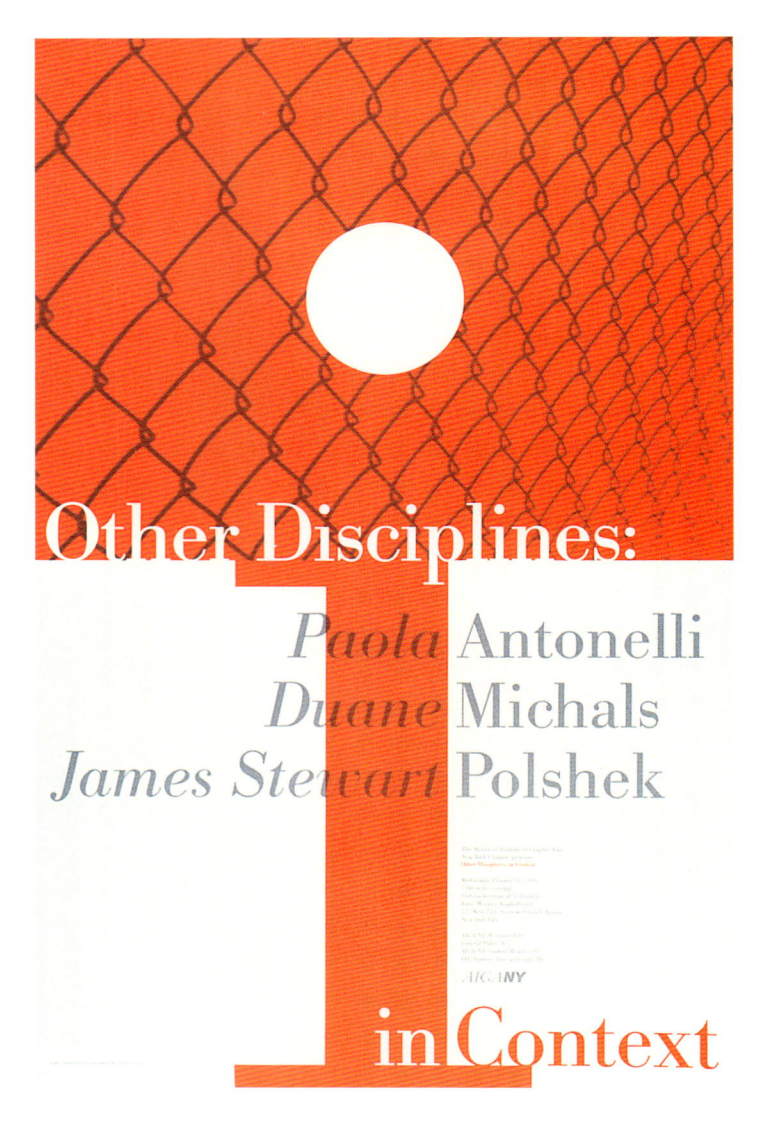

1. CD: Aoshi Kudo AD, D, I: Keiko Hirano CL: Shiseido Beauty Saloon Shibuya   Japan   1994

2. AD, D, P: J. Graham Hanson DF: J. Graham Hanson Design CL: American Institute of Graphic Arts / New York   USA   1995

POSTERS

1, 2. CD: Hiroyoshi Hidaka AD, D: Eiichi Sakota D, I: Toshio Kawakami DF: Rec 2nd CL: Hidaka Office   Japan   1994

3. AD, D, I: Kari Piippo DF: Kari Piippo OY CL: Volks Theater Rostock   Finland   1996

4. CD, AD, D: Michel Bouvet CL: Amnesty International   France   1993

54

2. AD, D, I: Katsunori Aoki CL: HB Gallery Japan 1993

1. AD, D, I: Gugi Akiyama CL: JAGDA Japan 1995

PRINTED MATERIAL

1. CD, AD, D, P, I: John Sayles CW: Wendy Lyons DF: Sayles Graphic Design CL: Continuum Healthcare   USA   1996

2. CD, AD, D, I: John Sayles D: Jennifer Elliott CW: Jack Jordison DF: Sayles Graphic Design CL: IMT   USA   1996

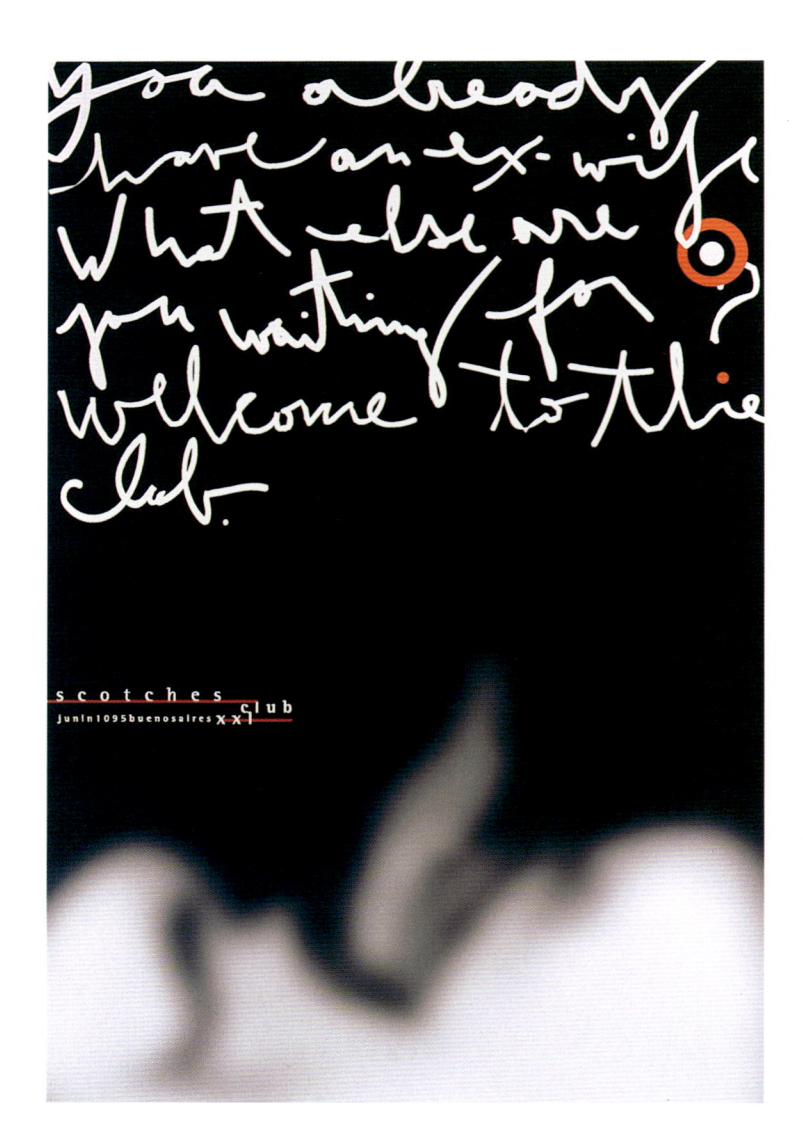

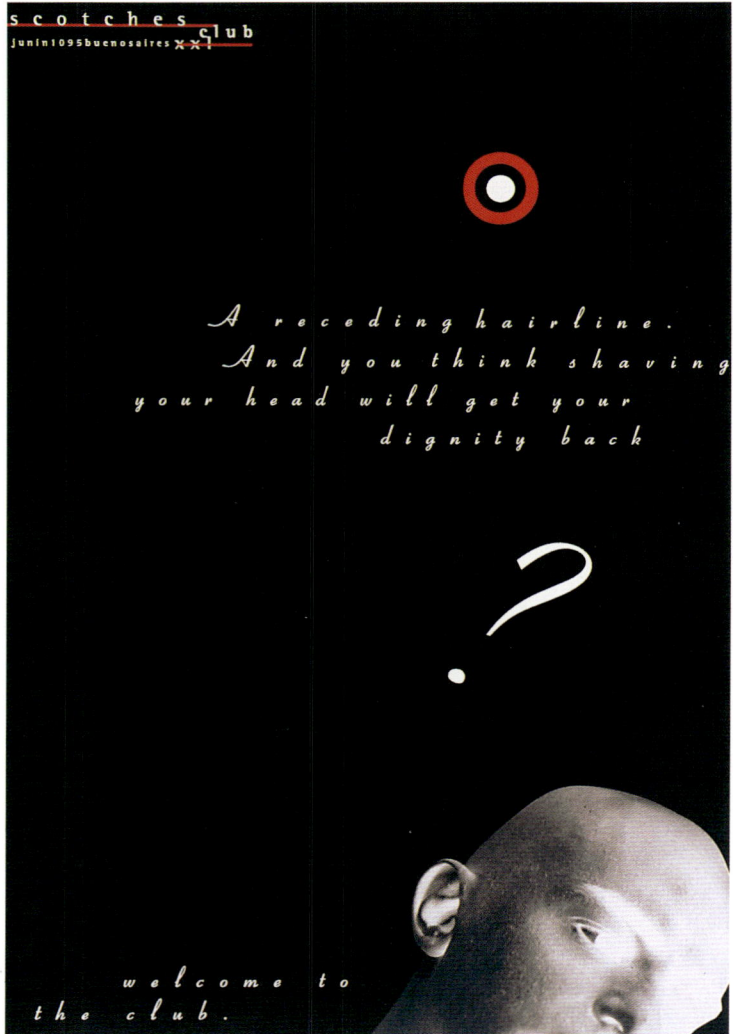

PRINTED MATERIAL

56   CD: Silvio Panizza   AD, D, P: Marcela Augustowsky   P: Guillermo Vega   CW: Fernanda Cava   DF: Pandora's Box   CL: Club XXI   Argentina   1994

CD, AD, D: Etsu CL: Feel Japan 1995

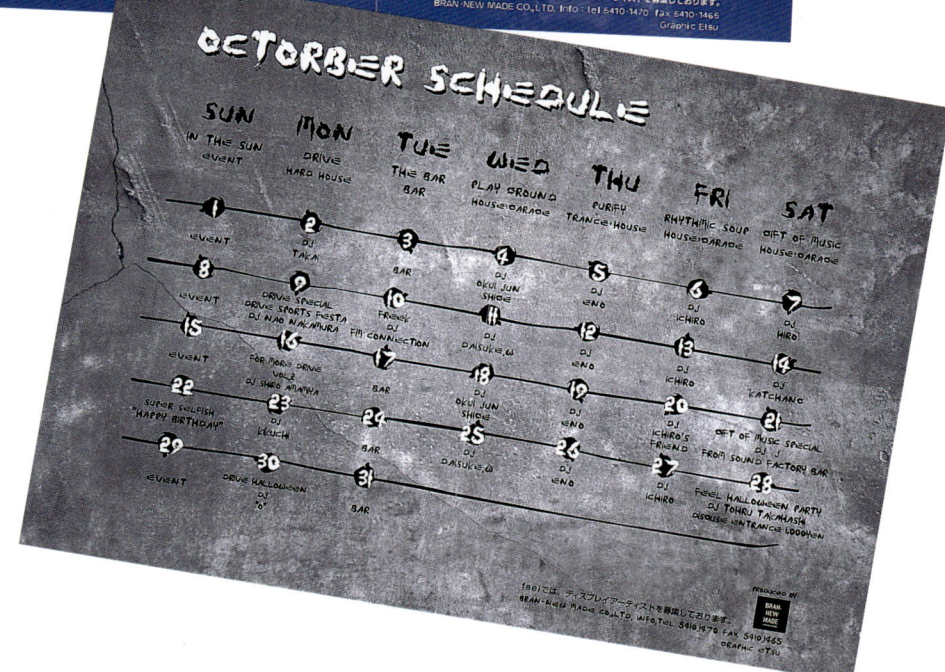

1. D, CL: Tsumori Chisato Japan 1996

2. CD, AD: Cinema Cats D: Masaharu Suzuki CL: Comstock Japan

PRINTED MATERIAL

1. D: Motoyuki Masaoka DF: Masaoka Graphics CL: Issey Miyake Inc. Japan 1996

2. CL: A-net Inc. Japan 1996

PRINTED MATERIAL

1, 3, 4. CD, AD, D: Makoto Orisaki CL: E & Y Co., Ltd. Japan 1995-1996
*4. Perforated ミシン目

2. CD, AD, D: Makoto Orisaki I: Michael Young CL: E & Y Co., Ltd. Japan 1995

PRINTED MATERIAL

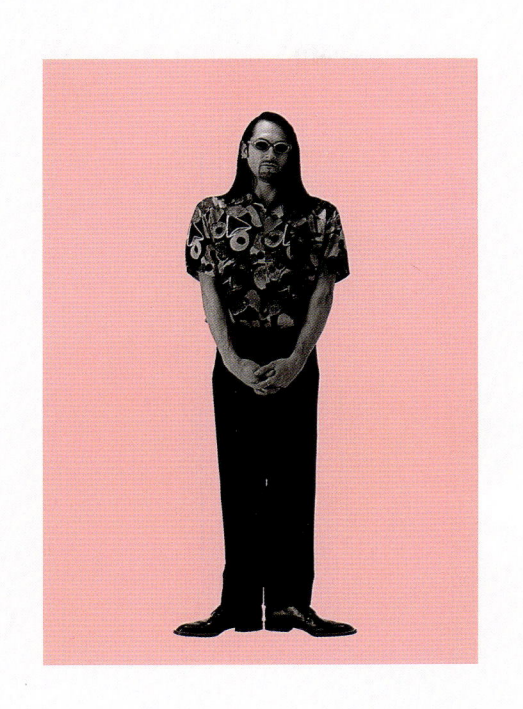

MONSIEUR
NICOLE
BY
YUKIO
KOBAYASHI

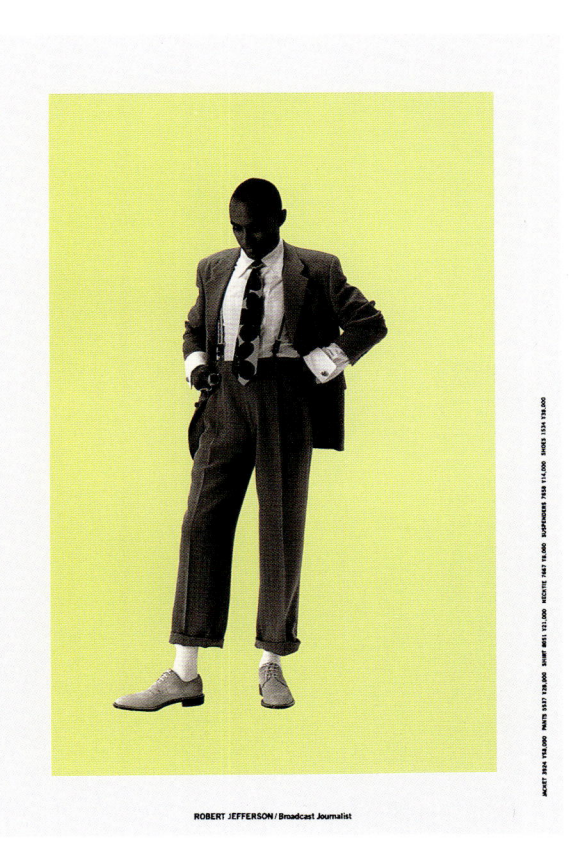

ROBERT JEFFERSON / Broadcast Journalist

AD: Hisao Sugiura D, DF: Studio Super Compass P: Naoaki Matsumoto CL: Nicole Co., Ltd. Japan 1996

PRINTED MATERIAL

1. CD: Troy Bailly D: Kathryn Lissack DF: Prototype Design CL: Arts Undergraduate Society of UBC Canada 1996

2. D: Troy Bailly / Stephen Parkes DF: Prototype Design CL: The Red Lounge Canada 1996

3. D: Stephen Parkes DF: Prototype Design CL: Starfish Room Canada 1994

PRINTED MATERIAL

1. AD, I: Kees Wagenaars DF: Case CL: Teater '77 Netherlands 1996

2. D: Kees Wagenaars DF: Case CL: Teejatergroep Orion Netherlands 1994

3. D: Kees Wagenaars DF: Case CL: Teater '77 Netherlands 1995

CD, AD, D, I, CW: Andrew Holland / Daniel Holliday DF: Trouble CL: The Sausage Machine UK 1989-1994

65

PRINTED MATERIAL

1. CD: Marcia Romanuck D: Alison Scheel / Fran McKay DF: The Design Company CL: Center for Puppetry Arts   USA   1995-1996

2. D: Kazuo Abe I: Yoko Tanimoto CL: The Room   Japan   1996

3. D, P: Kazuo Abe DF: Rhythmic Garden   Japan   1996

PRINTED MATERIAL

1. CD, AD, D, I, CW: Rvvd Van Empel DF: Van Den Beginne BV CL: Stichting Animatie Netherlands 1992

2. CD, AD, D, I: Troy M. Litten CW: Yolanda Edwards DF: Active White Space CL: 1015 Folsom USA 1994

67

1. D: Takao Yamashita Typographer: Simon Taylor CL: Beauty and Beast Japan 1996

2. D: Takao Yamashita CL: Beauty and Beast Japan 1992

3. D: Takao Yamashita P: Schoerner CL: Beauty and Beast Japan 1994

PRINTED MATERIAL

THE *GEE*STREET EXTRAVAGANZA 95'
Big Daddy
ITS On!

MUSIC BY FLIP SQUAD'S OWN **THE SUPREME BIGGA NIGGA KAP** OF HOT 97
HOSTED BY **REG REG** GUEST OF HONOR **THE PIMP PROMOTER SINCERE**

än-áb-wesend

07.06.96 – 15.06.96
Kulturfabrik Kofmehl Gibelinstrasse 15 Solothurn
Ein Kunstprojekt von Stek AG & Weltschmertz Neo Deo

1. **CD:** Ziggi Golding **AD, D:** David Calderley **CW:** Reg Reg **CL:** Gee Street Records   USA   1995

2. **AD, D:** Lopetz **P:** Stek Ag **DF:** Büro Destruct **CL:** Kulturfabrik Kofmehl   Switzerland   1996

PRINTED MATERIAL

1. AD, D: Sachi Sawada DF: "Moss" Design Unit CL: Nerd Japan 1996

2. AD, D: Lopetz DF: Büro Destruct CL: ISC Switzerland 1996

3, 4. AD, D: Marc Bastard Brunner DF: Büro Destruct CL: Markthalle Bern Switzerland 1996

PRINTED MATERIAL

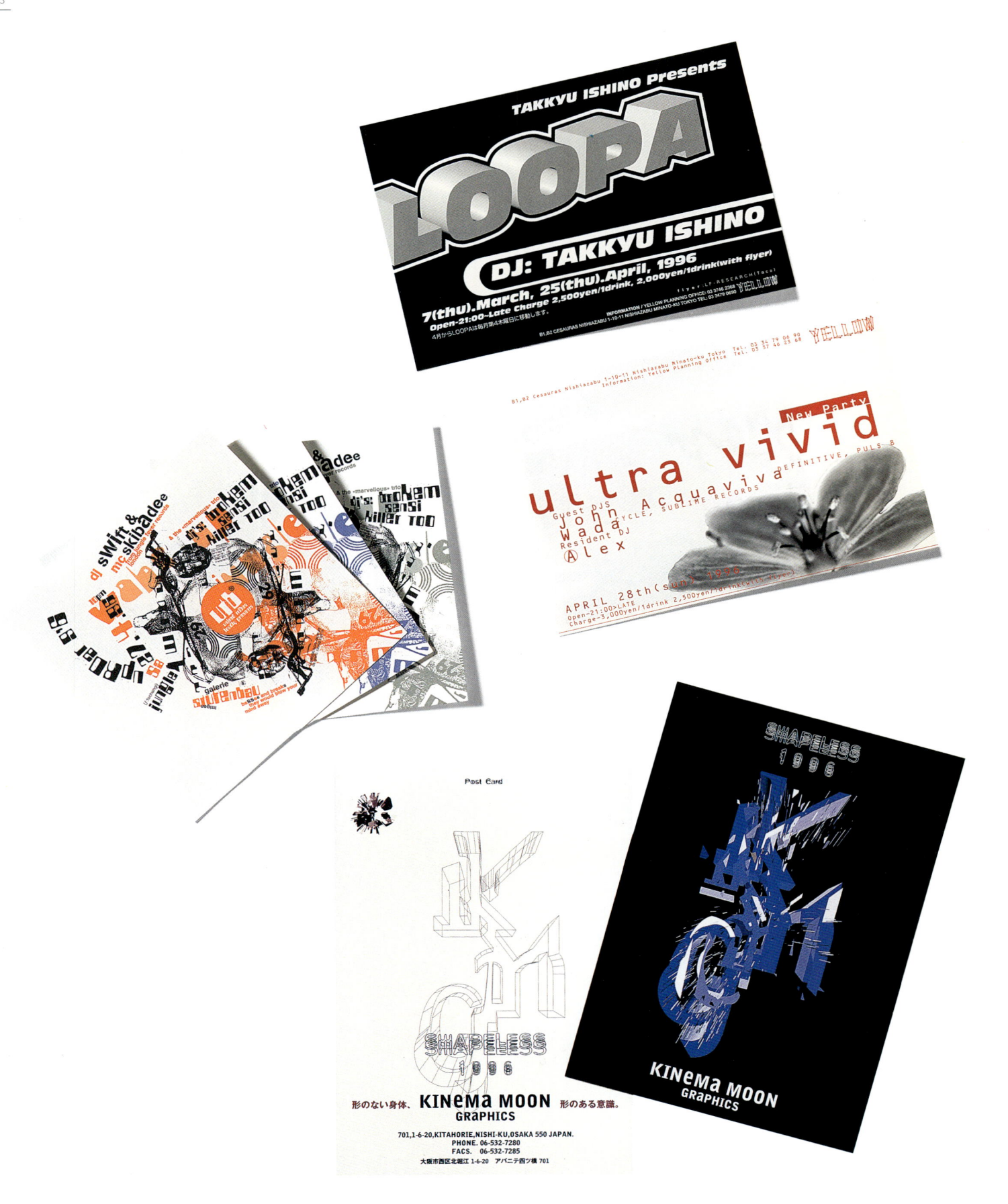

1. 3. AD, D: Takayuki Ichige DF: Hal Corporation CL: Ground Level Groove Japan 1996

2. AD, D, Faxcollage: Lopetz DF: Büro Destruct CL: United Tribes Switzerland 1996

4. AD: Yuichi Nakagawa D: Sachiko Kitani DF, CL: Kinema Moon Graphics Japan 1995

PRINTED MATERIAL

1. CD, AD: Retarded Whore D: Mark Damian / Christian Coffman   USA 1995

72

2. D, I: Sandy Gin DF, CL: Sandy Gin Design   USA 1996

3. CD: Jun Hatakeyama CL: Image Forum   Japan 1995

1. CD: Mika Kojima / Masanao Takase   AD, D, I: Gugi Akiyama   CL: G-One., Inc.   Japan   1994

2. CD, D: Mikiko Shimizu   I: Rieko Mukai   CL: Tokyo Can Co., Ltd.   Japan   1994

3. CD, D, I: Takumi Iwase   AD: Keiji Sugiura   DF: Tokyo Guns   CL: Club Cover   Japan   1996

PRINTED MATERIAL

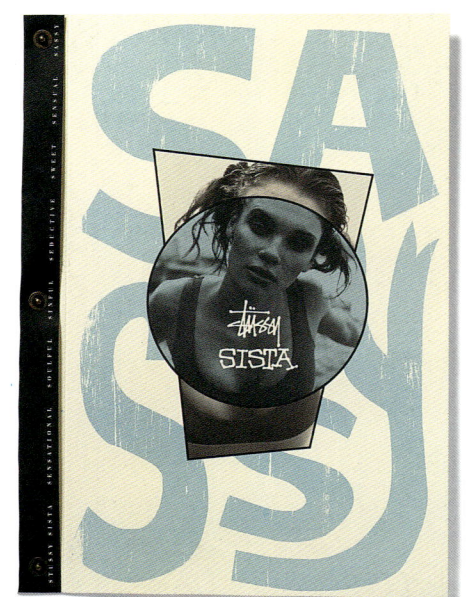

CD, AD, D: Andrew Hoyne DF: Andrew Hoyne Design CL: Stussy Sista Australia 1995

CD: Stuart I. Frolick D, P: Mike Fink DF, CL: Art Center College of Design USA 1994

PRINTED MATERIAL

THE TEN MOST ASKED QUESTIONS AND THEIR ANSWERS

NUMBER ONE — When will the **MGB SERVICE** be introduced? The service will commence from **May 1995**.

2. WHO WILL OWN THE MGB? NAWMA will have ownership of the bin and will deliver it to your home prior to commencement of the service.

HOW MANY bins can be serviced per household? **ONE BIN**, issued by NAWMA, will be serviced per household **EACH WEEK**.

4. WILL RESIDENTS HAVE TO PAY a deposit or the cost of the bin up front? There will be no direct charge on the bin.

5. What if the bin is damaged or stolen? Providing that residents have not been negligent, NAWMA will replace the bin at no cost.

6. What if a householder wishes to have a 240 litre bin or to change their 140 litre bin with a 240 litre bin at a later date? The householder will be required to pay a service fee of $50 p.a.

7. What if a resident selects a 240 litre bin and then wishes to replace it with a 140 litre bin at a later date? NAWMA will exchange it for a 140 litre bin at no cost to the Resident.

8. What if the household already ow[ns a 240] litre bin and wishes to contin[ue the] 240 litre service? Simply exchange your bin for a new one [and will] not be charged the $50 service fee for [the year.]

What if the householder does not [want] or use the bin supplied by NA[WMA for the] collection service? Only waste placed in the bin su[pplied] will be collected.

Can the householder pay a [fee for] an extra bin for collection? No, because the City toget[her with NAWMA wishes] to encourage hous[eholders to] home compost and parti[cipate in waste] reduction programs.

| NAWMA HOTLINE | PH: 250 8910 |
| CITY of MUNNO PARA | PH: 254 0123 |

mayor's message

The City of Munno Para is committed to reduce, reuse and recycle programs in waste management. Council encourages residents to recycle as much as possible. By composting kitchen scraps, leaves, lawn cuttings and other green waste, we can all help reduce the growing problems of waste disposal.

Waste collection for the City is contracted through the Northern Adelaide Waste Management Authority, known as NAWMA.

NAWMA is soon to replace the current waste collection service with Mobile Garbage Bins, commonly known as MGBs.

The new 140 litre MGBs will provide a safer and more convenient means of containing, moving and disposing of household waste.

This brochure will answer your initial questions about this new and improved service.

Council is confident this service will benefit all residents and we look forward to working with the community as we continue to develop greater services for the citizens of the City of Munno Para.

MAYOR
Jo Gapper
OAM JP

A MESSAGE FROM THE CHAIRMAN OF THE NORTHERN ADELAIDE WASTE MANAGEMENT AUTHORITY

Cr. Martin Lindsell, JP
CHAIRMAN NAWMA

NAWMA promotes safe and efficient waste collection and disposal and encourages waste minimisation practices. To encourage this, NAWMA supports the introduction of a 140 litre Mobile Garbage Bin (MGB) service to every household in the City of Munno Para.

THE THREE MAIN REASONS why we should minimise waste:

1) Reduce demand on raw materials such as trees.
2) Reduce volume of waste going to landfill which will assist in stabilising costs.
3) Support good environment and ecological practices.

WHY USE 140 LITRE BINS?

140 litre MGBs will help reduce the amount of waste going to landfill, stabilise costs, save trees and other raw materials, and help protect our sensitive environment.

We believe a 140 litre MGB is adequate for most households. It has a capacity of 20 kg which is about 9 kg more than the average weight of waste currently collected from homes.

NAWMA is also considering providing you with extra MGBs in the future to cater for both **recyclable** and **green** waste.

I urge you to support the introduction of 140 litre MGBs and encourage your family to use them correctly.

76

CD, AD: Alexander Musson D: Timothy Murphy DF: Poagi® CL: City of Munno Para   Australia 1994

PRINTED MATERIAL

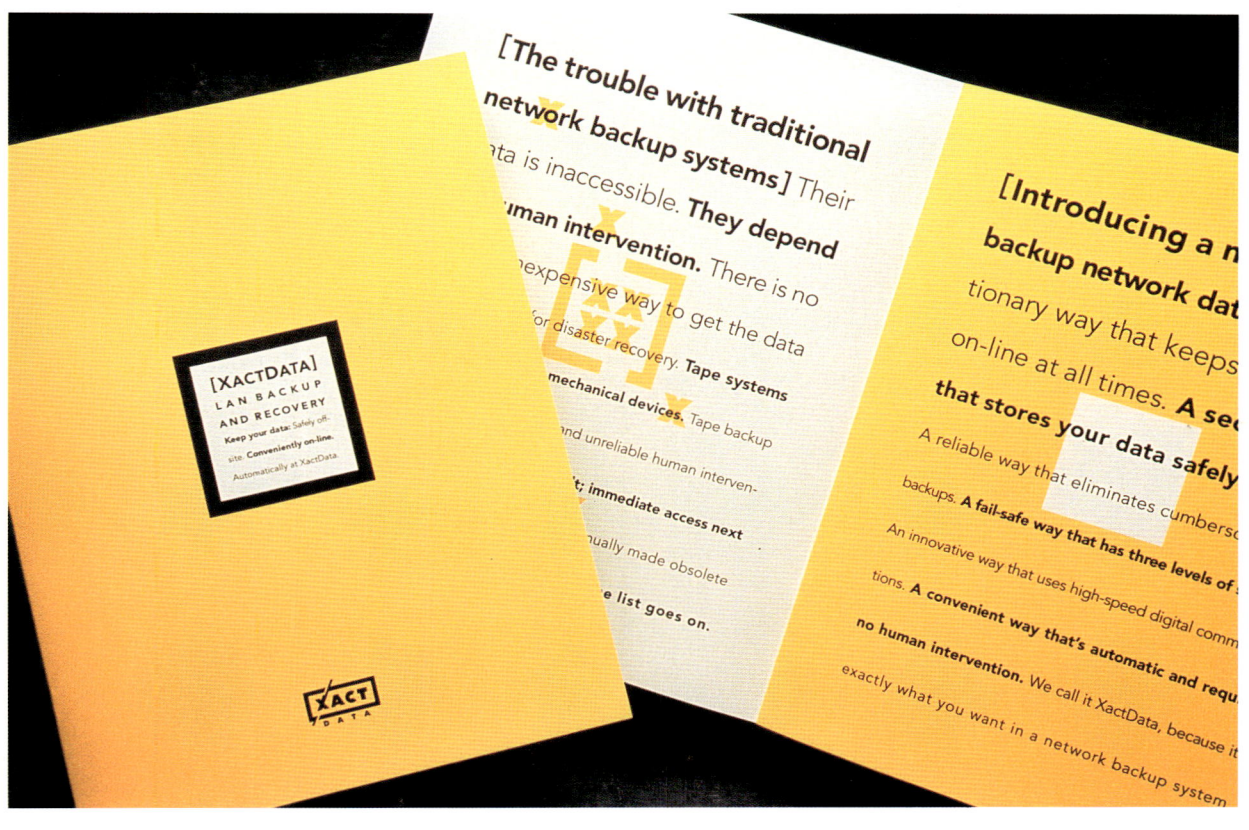

1. CD, AD: Sonia Greteman AD, D, I: James Strange CL: The Wichita Center for the Arts   USA 1996

2. AD, D: Jack Anderson D: Lisa Cerveny / Jana Wilson / Julie Keenan CW: Jeff Fraga DF: Hornall Anderson Design Works CL: Xact Data Corporation   USA 1995

PRINTED MATERIAL

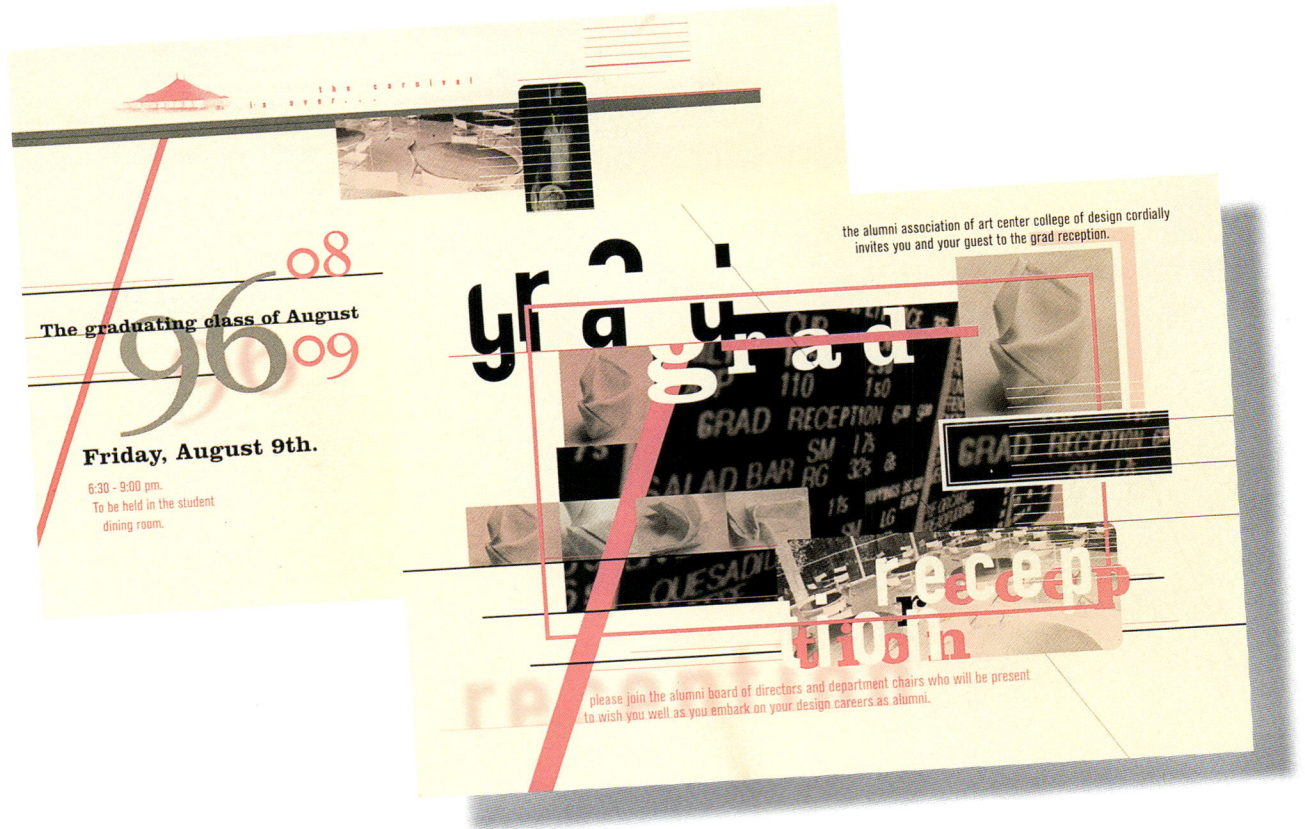

1. **D:** Daniel R. Smith **DF:** NBBJ Graphic Design **CL:** NBBJ   USA   1996

2. **CD:** Stuart I. Frolick **AD:** Darin Beaman **D:** Thomas Muller **P:** Steven A. Heller **DF, CL:** Art Center College of Design   USA   1995

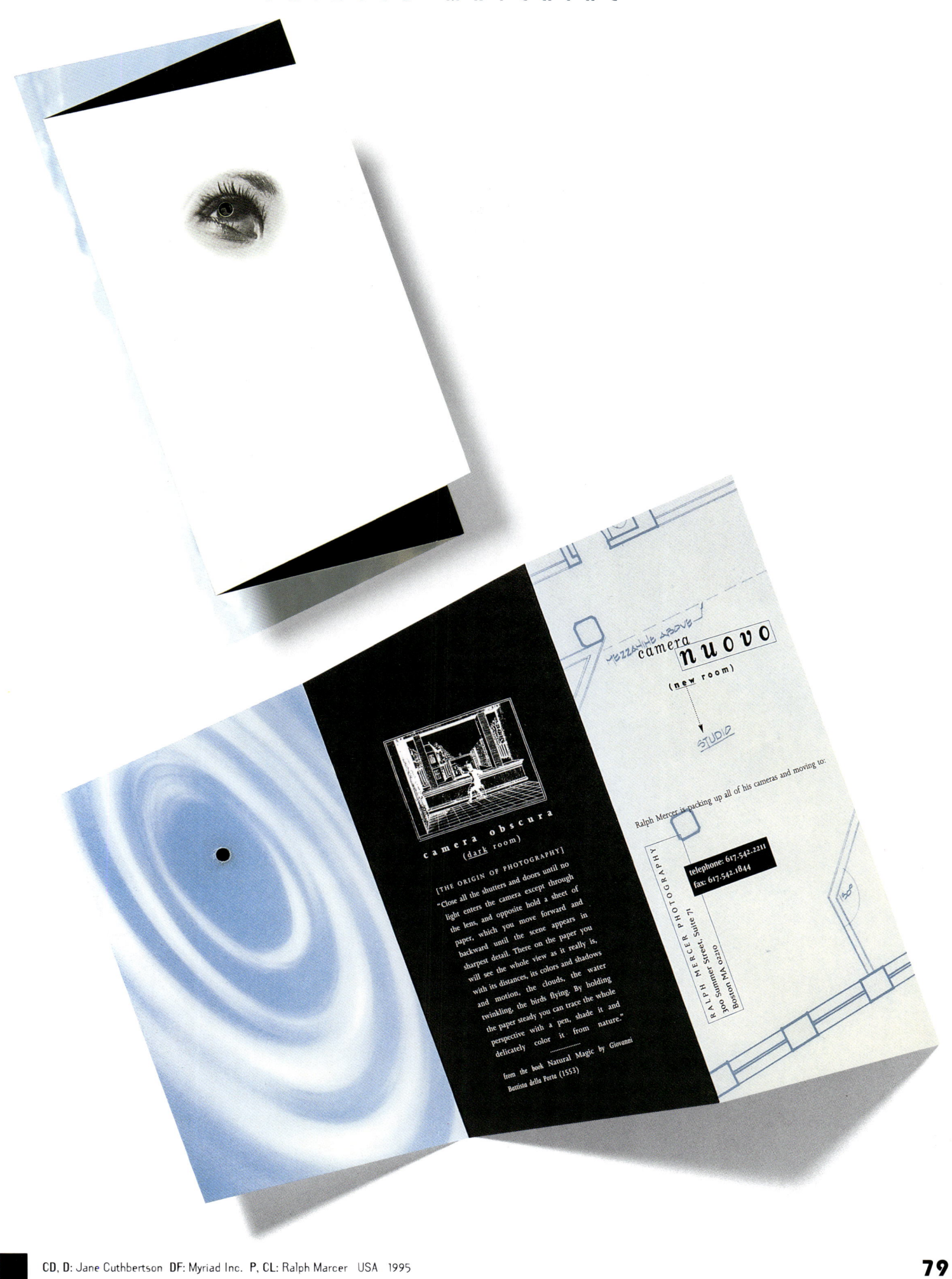

CD, D: Jane Cuthbertson DF: Myriad Inc. P, CL: Ralph Mercer   USA   1995

PRINTED MATERIAL

1. PD: Junji Ito CD: Shigeru Yamaoka AD: Keiji Ito D: Yoshiko Okamoto DF: Studio Give / Lop Lop Design Inc. Japan 1993

2. AD, D: Takeshi Kuroda P: Miwa Isoi DF: Office Sandscape CL: Planet Pistaccio Japan 1995

3. CD, AD, D, P: Pascal Béjean DF, CL: Bleu Élastique France 1995

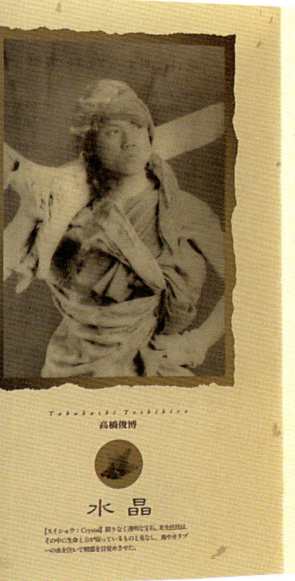

PRINTED MATERIAL

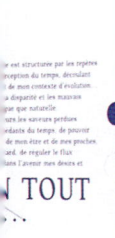

1. **AD:** Ric Riordon **D:** Sharon Pece **I:** Dan Wheaton **DF:** The Riordon Design Group Inc. **CL:** Samsung Electronics Canada   Canada 1995

2. **CD:** Carlos Segura **AD, D, I:** Laura Alberts **DF:** Segura Inc. **CL:** MRSA   USA 1996

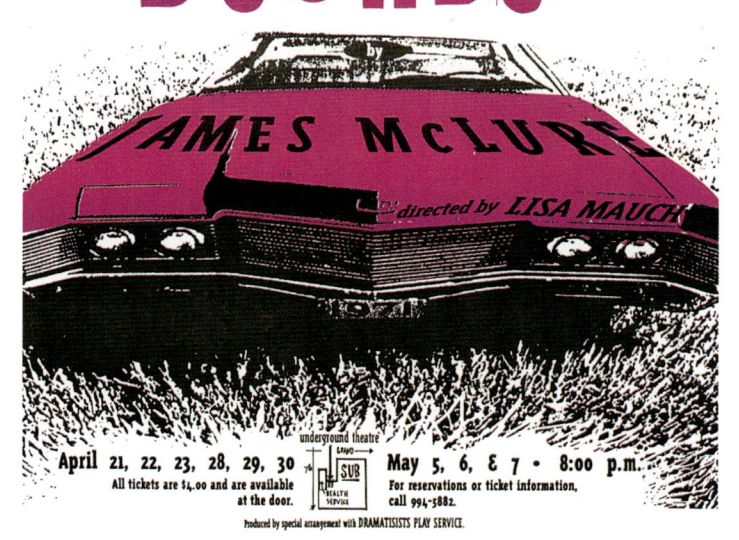

1. AD, D, I: George Estrada DF: Modern Dog CL: Tasty Shows USA 1995

2. CD: Lisa Mauch AD, D, I: Coby Schultz DF: Modern Dog CL: Underground Theatre USA 1994

PRINTED MATERIAL

Arterit
Integrate color idiom

1. How should walls of new office be?
2. What color should wall be to make the office look comfortable?
3. What is the most suitable wall color for this floor color?
4. Would you like to participate in color planning of your office?
5. Would you like to renovate your showroom?
⑥ Arterit answers all of the above questions.
⑦ Arterit supports office renovation with its concept of "integrated color idiom."

series 900

1. AD, D: Yasuhiro Sawada CL: Nippon Paint Co., Ltd. Japan 1992

2. AD, D: Clifford Stoltze D: Wing Ip Ngan Typography: Richard Leighton DF: Stoltze Design CL: Castle von Buhler Records USA 1996

FALL/WINTER 1996
MATSUDA
COLLECTION
FOR WOMEN AND MEN
BY YUKIO
KOBAYASHI

AD, D: Hideki Nakajima CL: Nicole Co., Ltd. Japan 1996

PRINTED MATERIAL

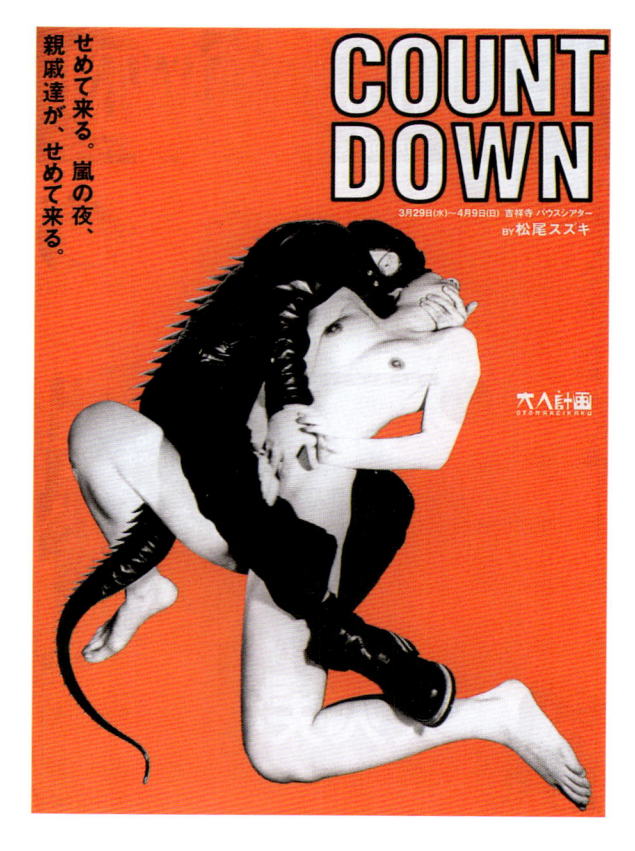

1, 2. D: Shoji Tsumura CL: R·C·S Japan 1. 1996 / 2. 1995

3. CD: Akihiro Suzuki AD, D: Yasunori Arai DF: Picture Disc CL: Stance Company Japan 1992

4. CD: Suzuki Matsuo AD, D: Masami Yoshizawa P: Junsuke Takimoto CL: Otona Keikaku Japan 1995

PRINTED MATERIAL

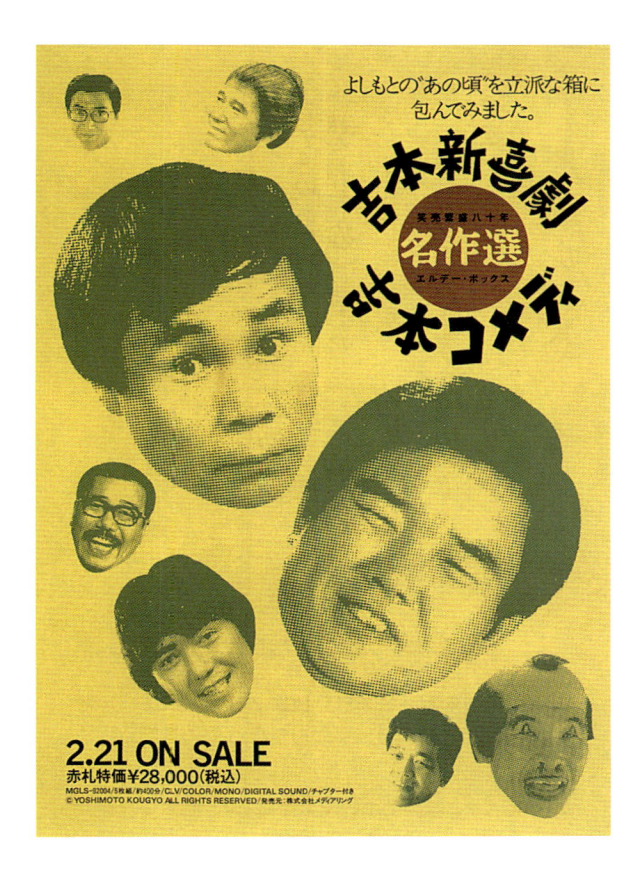

1, 2. CD, AD, D, I: Toru Kunugida DF: Never Land CL: Media Rings Corporation Japan 1992

3. AD, D, I: Sachi Sawada DF: "Moss" Design Unit Japan 1996

4. CD: Keralino Sandrovich AD, D: Masashi Komura D: Chisako Amazutsumi P: Chikako Kamitori CL: Silly Walk Co., Ltd. Japan 1996

87

語り合う
インフォームド・コンセント
患者のおもい 医療者のこころ

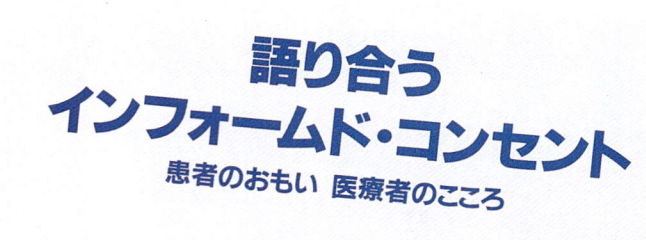

第4回COML医療フォーラム／1995年9月3日(日)10:00am→5:00pm／ドーンセンター

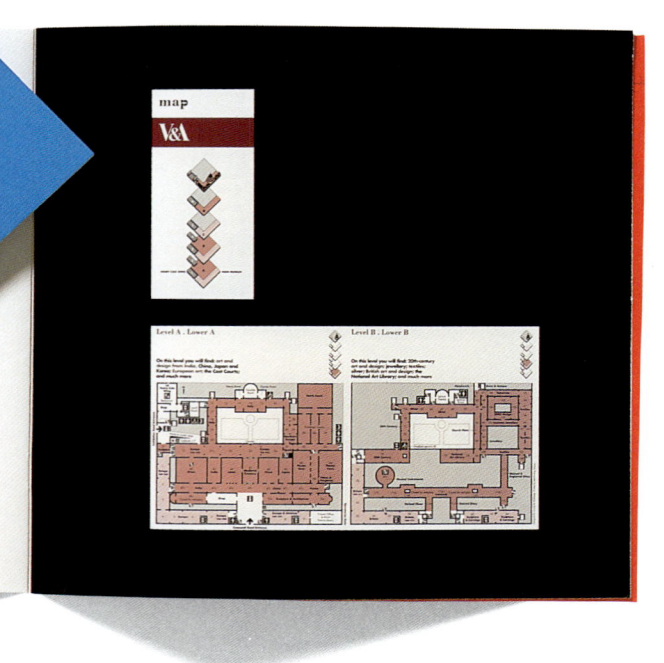

1. D, I: Shotaro Manabe CL: Coml Japan 1995

2. CD, D: Peter Grundy CD: Tilly Northedge DF, CL: Grundy & Northedge UK 1995

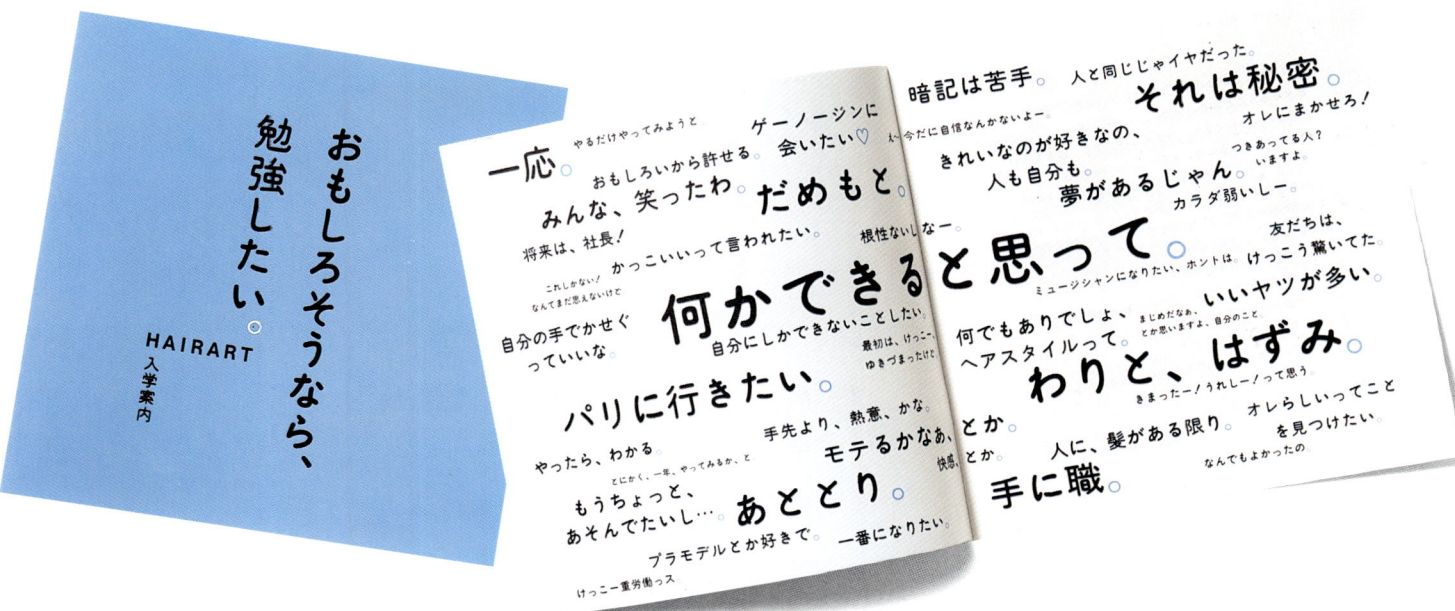

PRINTED MATERIAL

1. CD, AD, D: Hiroaki Konya DF, CL: Kokoku Nojyo Japan 1995

2. CD: Atsuhiro Miyakawa AD, D: Eiichi Sakota CW: Keiko Sato DF: Rec 2nd CL: Hairart Japan 1996

PRINTED MATERIAL

1. CD, AD: Jim Christie I: Isabelle Dervaux DF, CL: Jim Christie Design USA 1996
2. AD, I: Isabelle Dervaux CL: C. W. C. USA 1996

SEASON'S GREETINGS

1. AD: Katsumi Komagata D: Aki Ishijima DF: One Stroke Co., Ltd. CL: Still Waters Japan 1996

2. AD: Katsumi Komagata D: Aki Ishijima DF, CL: One Stroke Co., Ltd. Japan 1995

CD: Suzuki Matsuo AD, D: Masami Yoshizawa P: Junsuke Takimoto I: Yoshiharu Mitsumoto CL: Otona Keikaku Japan 1996

1. CD: Masaaki Kato AD, D: Eiichi Sakota D: Yoshitaka Shinmori
D, I: Toshio Kawakami DF: Rec 2nd CL: FM Osaka Japan 1996

2. CD, AD, D: Hiroaki Konya DF: Kokoku Nojo CL: Mitsuaki Shibuya Japan 1995

HERRON GALLERY
Indianapolis Center for Contemporary Art

CLAYFEST No. 8

A Juried Biennial of

INDIANA CERAMIC ARTISTS

and

AMACO SELECTS: TEN YEARS OF CERAMIC WORKSHOPS

DECEMBER 5, 1992 – JANUARY 8, 1993

HERRON SCHOOL OF ART
1701 N. PENNSYLVANIA ST.
INDIANAPOLIS, IN. 46202
317 920-2420

MONDAY – THURSDAY
10:00 AM TO 7:00 PM
FRIDAY 10:00 AM TO 5:00 PM

These exhibitions are funded in part by The Mary Howes Woodsmall Foundation, American Art Clay Co., Inc., the Friends of Herron, the Indiana Arts Commission and the National Endowment for the Arts.

PRINTED MATERIAL

October comes in like a lamb and goes out like a lion.

↓こどもを うむ へやは くらく して やります。

こどもを うむ へや

1. CD, I: Senri Imada AD, D, CL: Sachi Sawada DF: "Moss" Design Unit Japan 1996

2. CD, AD, D: Issay Kitagawa I: Mar Sekiguchi CL: Japan Design Committee Japan 1996

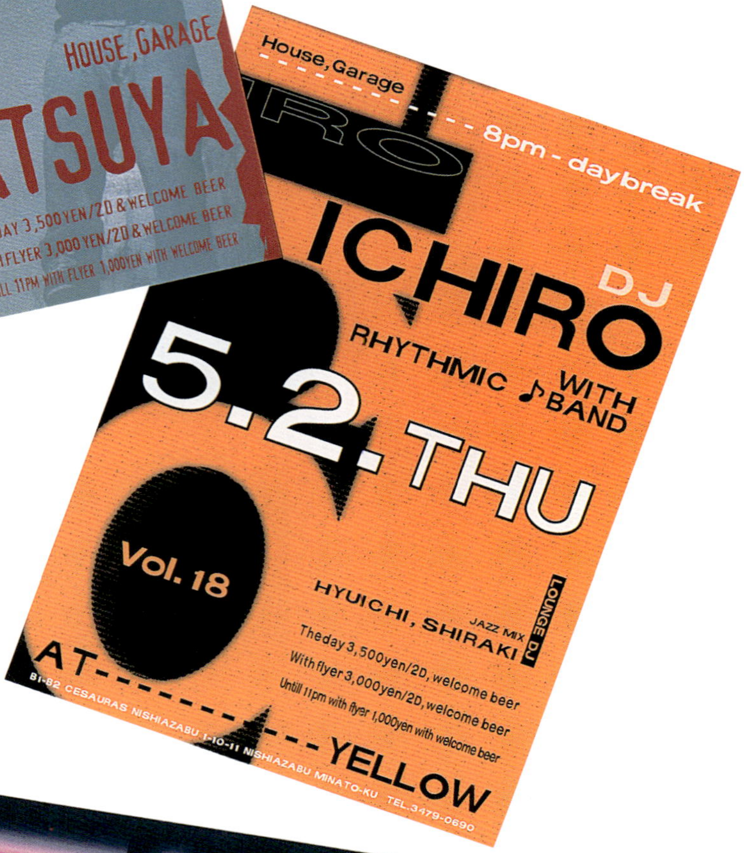

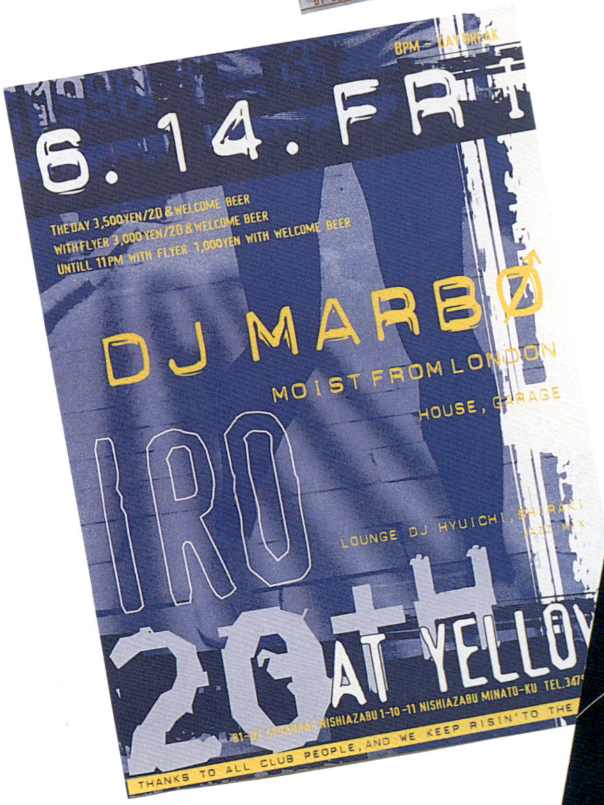

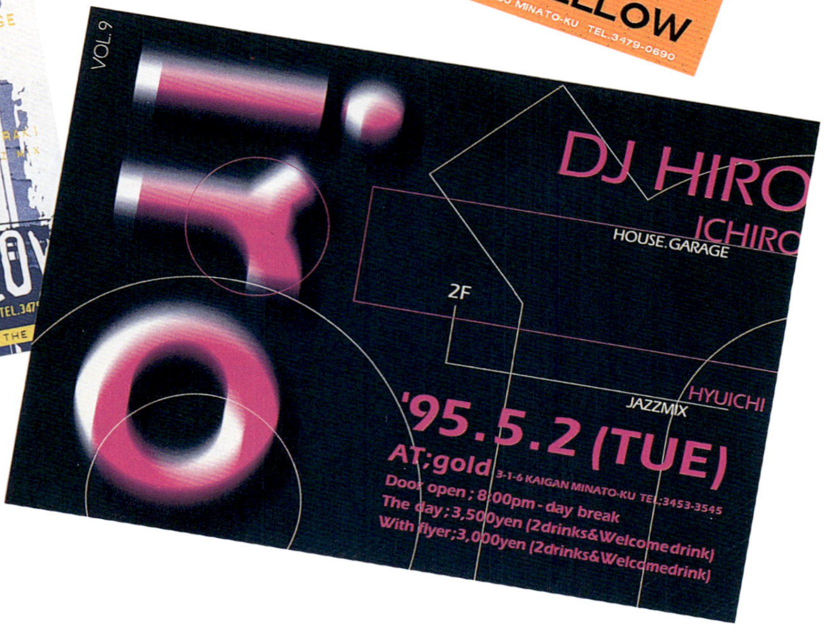

CD, AD, D: Etsu CL: Bran-New Made Co., Ltd. Japan 1995

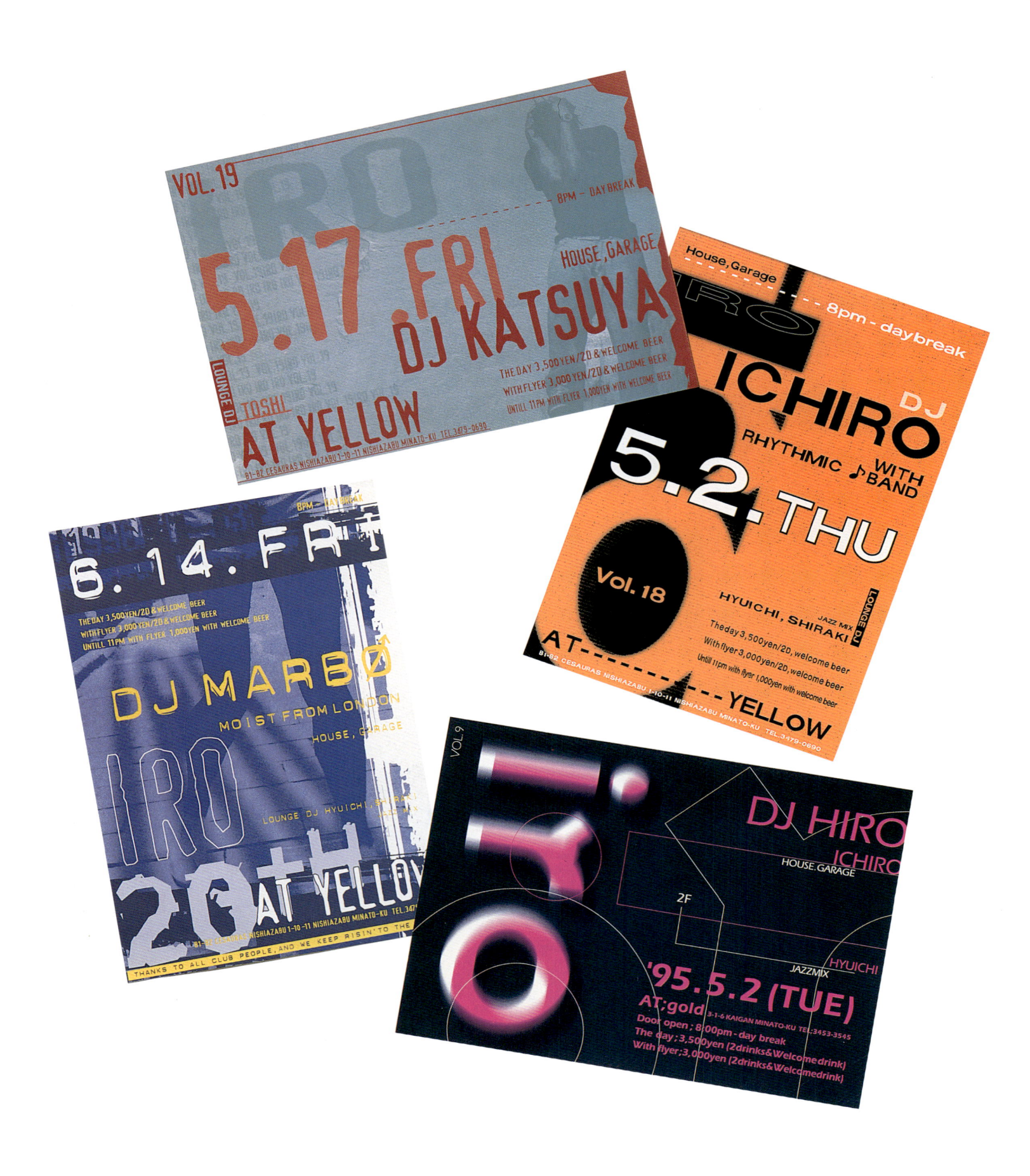

1. CD: G-Works AD, D, P: Mitsuyuki Odajima CL: Logic   Japan   1996

2. AD, D: Akira Sumi CL: Hiroshige Maki Atelier   Japan   1996

1. **AD, D:** Yasushi Kikuchi **Editor:** Yoichi Nakamuta (E & Y Co., Ltd.) / John Storey **CL:** E & Y Co., Ltd. Japan 1995

2. **AD, D:** Haruki Mori **DF:** Azone + Associates **CL:** T2 Japan 1996

PRINTED MATERIAL

1. D: Takashi Sasaki CL: Dual Growing System Inc. Japan 1996

2. CD, AD, D: J. J. F. G. Borrenbergs / R. Verkaart DF: Stoere Binken Design CL: Sirius Netherlands 1996

3. CD, D: Yasushi Okumura AD: Naoki Kihira CL: Karma Japan 1995

PRINTED MATERIAL

100

1. CD, AD, D: Ross McBride DF, CL: Designatorium Japan 1994

2. CD, AD, D, P: Clifford Cheng DF, CL: Voice Design USA 1996

PRINTED MATERIAL

1. AD: Charles Shields D: Juan Vega DF, CL: Shields Design   USA   1993

2. AD, D: Haruki Mori DF: Azone + Associates   Japan   1996

PRINTED MATERIAL

1. AD, D: Katsunori Aoki CL: Peace Card Japan 1995

102

2. AD, D: Katsunori Aoki I, CL: Akemi Suetsugu Japan 1994

3. AD, D: Katsunori Aoki CL: HB Gallery Japan 1996

PRINTED MATERIAL

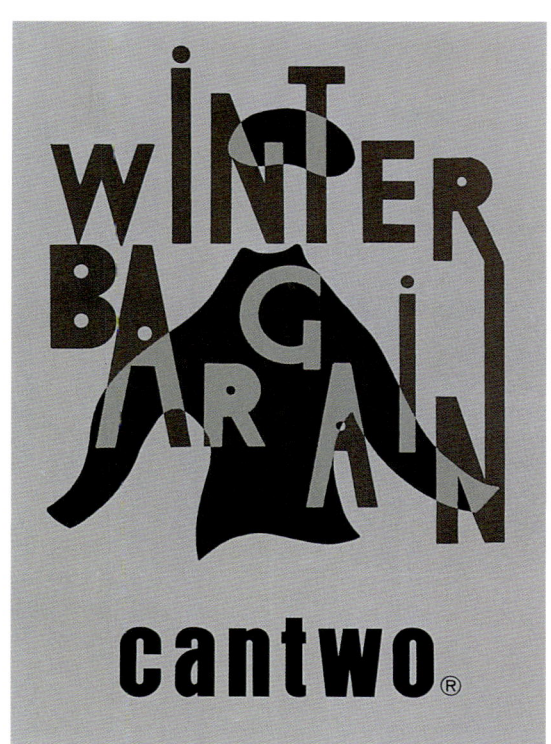

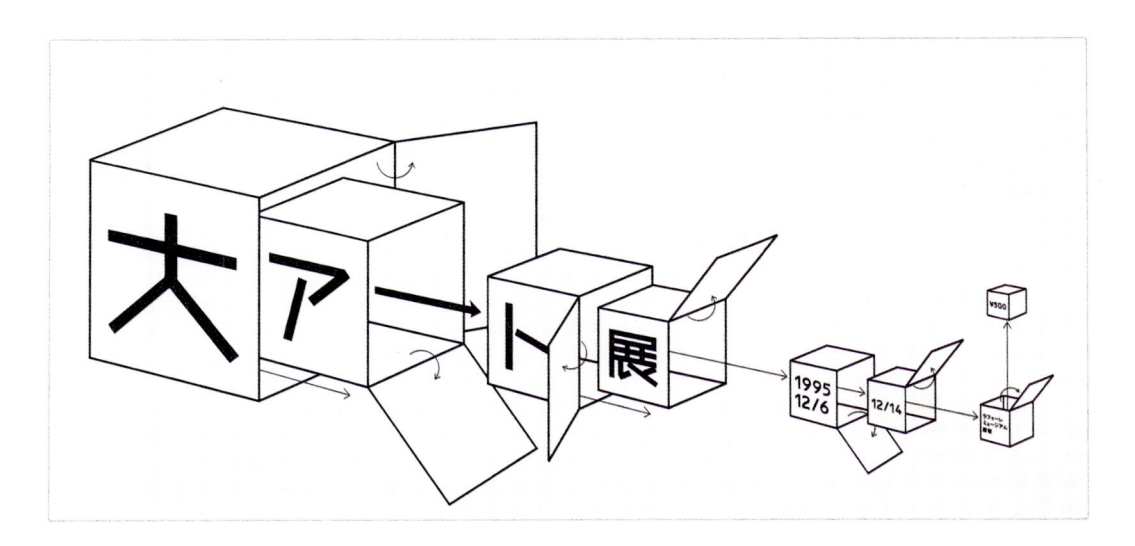

1. CD, D: Keiko Watanabe CL: Tokyo Can Co., Ltd. Japan 1996

2. D, I: Shotaro Manabe CL: Go-Go Project Japan 1996

3. AD: Norio Nakamura D: Hiromi Watanabe CL: Sony Music Entertainment (Japan) Inc. Japan 1995
*Varnish

1. CD: Chris H. Sekine AD, D: Noriyoshi Kawahara I: Katsuyuki Nishizuka CL: Yellow Japan 1996

2. CD, AD, D: Hiroaki Doi CL: Uichi Yamamoto Japan 1994

1. CD: Noli-Pee AD, I: Stupid CL: Mushroom   Japan 1995

2. CD: Noli-Pee AD: Stupid CL: Mushroom   Japan 1995

3. CD, AD: Stupid CL: Club Karma   Japan 1996

鬼才誕生40周年記念

ウメカニズム
UMECHANISM
前人未到の楳図かずお展

●レセプション・パーティのご案内●

春陽の候、皆様益々ご清祥のこととお慶び申し上げます。
この度ラフォーレ原宿では、
楳図かずお氏の作家デビュー40周年を記念し
「ウメカニズム──前人未到の楳図かずお展」を
開催するはこびとなりました。
一度読んだら脳裏に焼きついて離れない恐怖漫画から、
ハチャメチャなギャグ漫画、
そして壮大なスケールで展開するSF大作まで強烈で振幅を持った作品群、
また音楽活動やテレビ出演で見せるポップな個性は、
日本の漫画界・文化人の中でもまさに異脳（能）の鬼才として、
常に注目を集めています。
今回の展覧会は、選りすぐった300点近くの原画の展示、
ユニークな生活・仕事空間やステージ活動の紹介、
貴重な関係資料やグッズの展示など、
氏の40年にわたる活動の軌跡とパーソナリティを多角的に公開するものです。
また小学館より「ウメカニズム──楳図かずお大解剖」が同時期に発売され、
展覧会と相互補完的に、
この希有な創造者の現代における存在意義を明らかにしてゆきます。
4月21日、本展開催およびデビュー40周年を記念し、
下記要領でレセプションパーティを開催いたします。
当日は楳図氏のミニ・ステージも飛び出すかと思われます。
ご多忙中とは存じますが、皆様万障お繰り合わせのうえ
ご出席の栄を賜りたく、ご案内申し上げます。

1995年4月
ラフォーレ原宿

記

日時：1995年4月21日(金) 午後7時〜9時
会場：ラフォーレミュージアム原宿
東京都渋谷区神宮前1-11-6 ラフォーレ原宿6階
お問い合わせ：TEL.03-5411-3301 FAX.03-5411-3308 ラフォーレ原宿（担当/武村・田中）
●同封の返信ハガキを4月15日までにご投函ください。
●ご来場の際は本状封筒を会場受付へお示しください。
●プレス取材ご希望の方は、4月19日までにお電話またはFAXにて上記あてご連絡ください。

CD: Yukihiko Asano AD, D: Gugi Akiyama P: Takashi Homma Artist: Kazuo Umezu CL: Laforet Harajuku Japan 1995

1. AD, D, I: Simon Sernec CL: G Klub Slovenia 1991

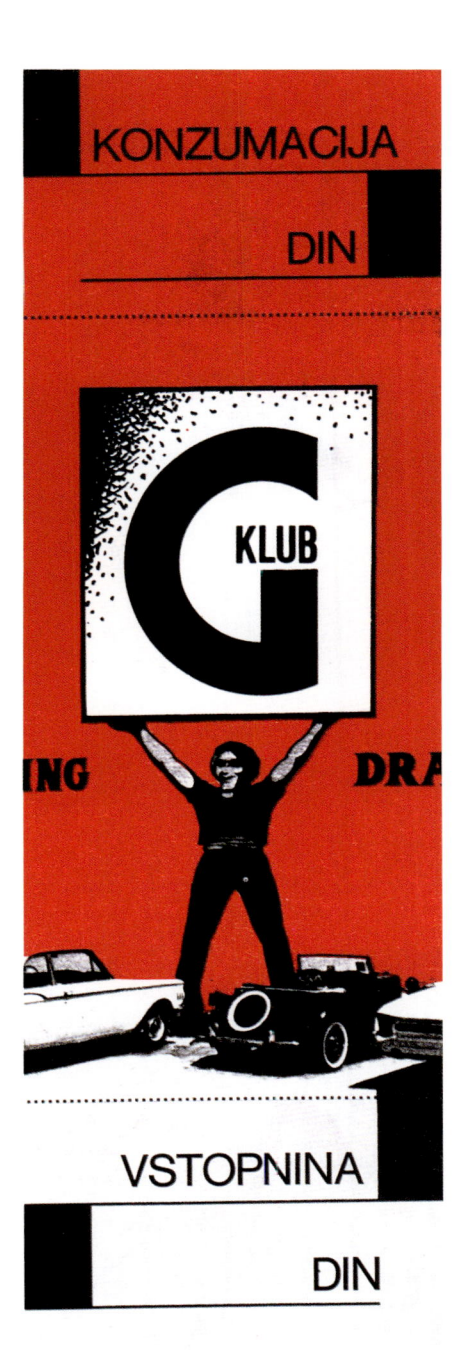

2. CD, AD, D: André ce Castro DF: Interface Designers CL: O Globo Newspaper Brazil

3. AD, D: Kenzo Izutani D: Aki Hirai DF: Kenzo Izutani Office Corp. CL: Parco Japan 1990

1. CD, D: Gonzalo Berro D: Macarena Ubios DF: Cato & Berro Diseño CL: Puente Mitre Argentina 1996

2. CD, D: Gonzalo Berro D: Esteban Serrano DF: Cato & Berro Diseño CL: Puente Mitre Argentina 1996

Tai-oan m-si Tiong-kok
Tai-oan hoan Tai-oan
Tiong-kok hoan Tiong-kok

Tai-oan hoan Tai-oan
Tiong-kok hoan Tiong-kok.
Hoan-tui tion-hoa-chu-gi

AD, D: Akira Utsumi P: Loe-hai, Chiong CL: Tai-gi-pan Japan 1996

1. AD, D: Takeshi Kuroda P: Miwa Isoi DF: Office Sandscape CL: Planet Pistaccio Japan 1994

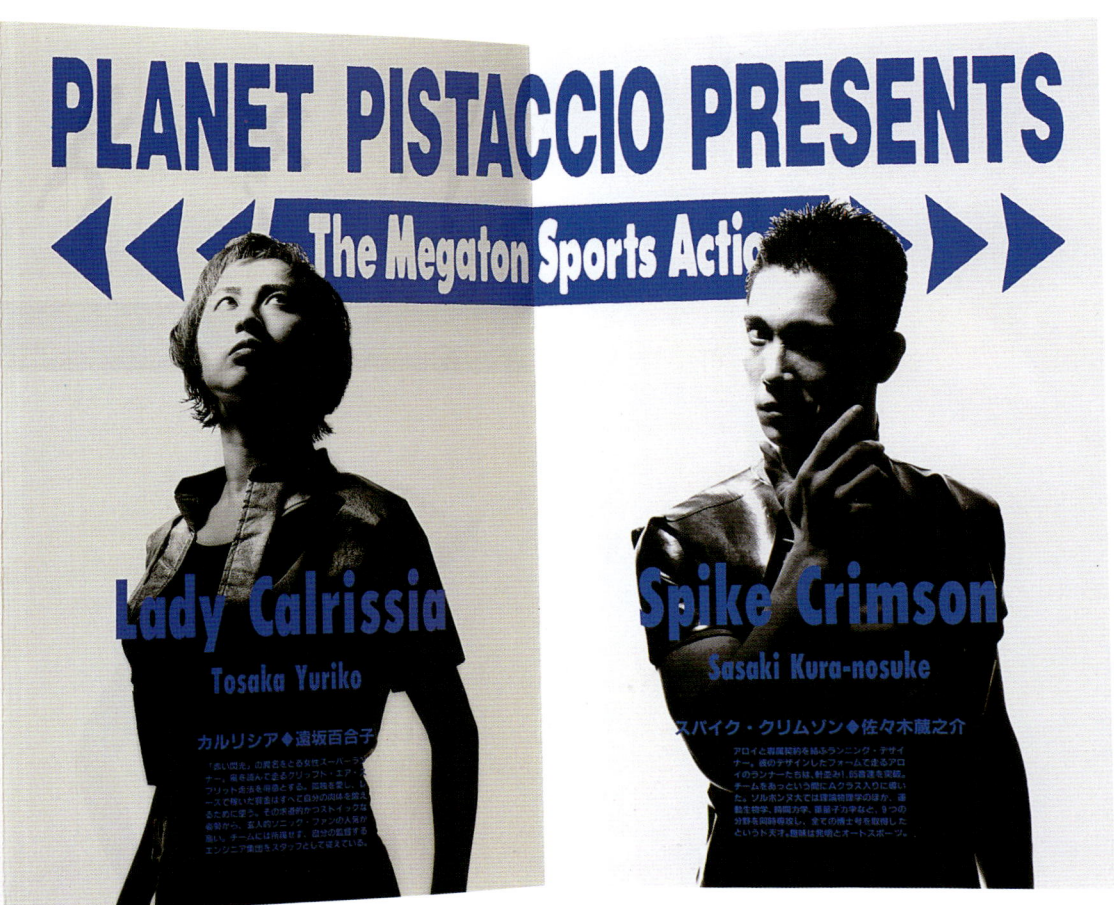

2. D: Stefanie Choi DF: NBBJ Graphic Design CL: Columbia Seafirst Center USA 1985

PRINTED MATERIAL

1. CD, AD, D: Leslie Chan Wing Kei D: Toto Tseng DF: Leslie Chan Design Co., Ltd. CL: Toppy Fashion Co., Ltd. Taiwan 1995

2. CD: Stuart I. Frolick AD, D: Darin Beaman I: Marla Frazee DF, CL: Art Center College of Design USA 1995

PRINTED MATERIAL

1. **CD, AD, D:** Sonia Greteman **AD, D:** James Strange **CL:** Duffens Optical   USA

2. **CD, D:** Mario A. Mirelez **DF:** Mirelez / Ross Inc. **CL:** Thomson Consumer Electronics   USA   1994

PRINTED MATERIAL

1. CD: Stuart I. Frolick AD: Darin Beaman D, P: Brian Rackleff DF, CL: Art Center College of Design USA 1995

2. AD, D: Shannon Beer CL: Shannon Beer / David Belanger USA 1996

PRINTED MATERIAL

1. **AD, D:** Clifford Stoltze **D:** Rebecca Fagan / Peter Farrell **DF, CL:** Stoltze Design USA 1993

2. **CD, D:** Jane Jenkins / Tom Jenkins **CW:** Jim Thackray **DF:** The Design Foundry **CL:** The Nature Conservancy USA 1995

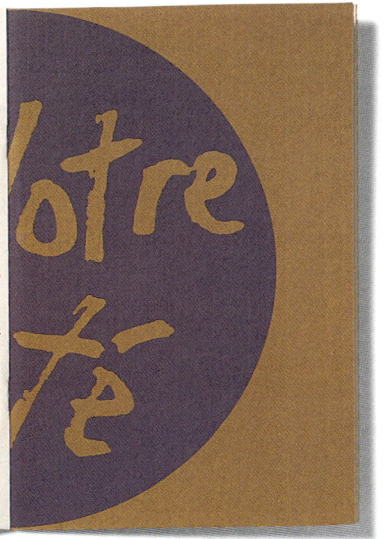

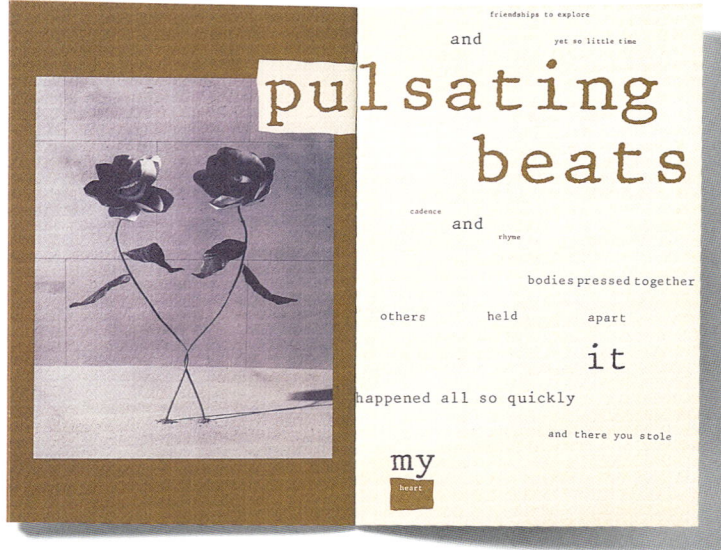

PRINTED MATERIAL

1. **AD, D:** Jeffrey Fabian / Laura Latham / Samuel Shelton **P:** Geof Kern **CW:** Cheryl P. Duvall
DF: Kinetik Communication Graphics, Inc. **CL:** Design Industries Foundation for AIDS, DC   USA 1991

2. **CD, AD:** Cinema Cats **D:** Masaharu Suzuki **CL:** Comstock   Japan

PRINTED MATERIAL

1
2
3

LEO BURNETT IS MOVING.

1. **CD, AD**: Stefan Sagmeister **D**: Veronica Oh **DF**: Sagmeister Inc.   USA   1993

2. **CD, AD**: Stefan Sagmeister **D, I**: Mike Chu **D**: Peter Rae / Patrick Daily **P**: Arthur Schulten **DF**: The Design Group **CL**: Leo Burnett   USA   1993

3. **CD, AD**: Stefan Sagmeister **D, I**: Susanne Poelleritzer **P**: Michael Grimm **DF**: Sagmeister Inc. **CL**: Fabrica   USA

PRINTED MATERIAL

118

1. AD, D: Shannon Beer P: Craig Bailey CL: Craig Hickman   USA 1995

2. AD: Ric Riordon D: Dan Wheaton / Shirley Riordon DF: The Riordon Design Group Inc. CL: University of Toronto   Canada 1996

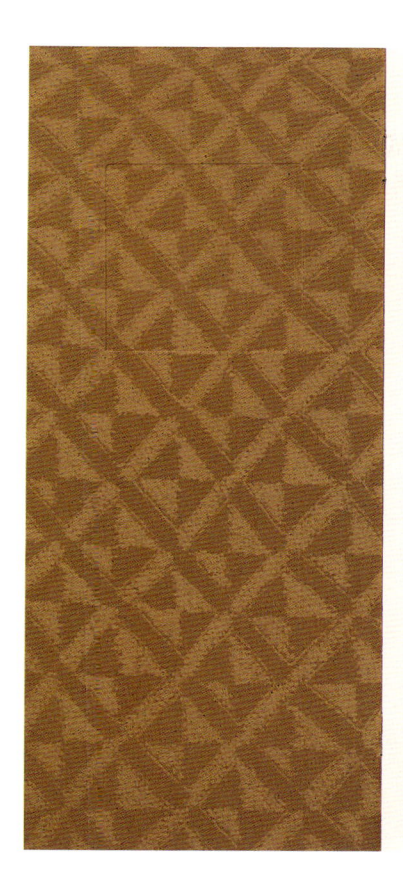

PRINTED MATERIAL

BELLEVUE CLUB HOTEL

For discriminating travelers, the Bellevue Club Hotel is a very special find: a hotel only minutes from all that matters... and a retreat that's dramatic yet quiet. ◆ It is, for appointments and detailing, a hotel on par with the best. For feeling, it is completely its own. ◆ Artistic and original... imaginative and rich...

Here, guests enjoy the privileges of membership in unparalleled social and athletic facilities.

BELLEVUE CLUB HOTEL

BELLEVUE CLUB HOTEL

Each one of our sixty-four rooms and three suites is unique, though they share an ambience that's intimate... refined. ◆ At every turn, you'll find an unexpected detail... an original touch. ◆ From handcrafted furniture, imported fabrics, and spa bath facilities in limestone and marble... whether overlooking the fountain court yard, tennis, or southerly vistas to Mt. Rainier, you are surrounded by substance, grace, and strength.

CD, AD, D: Leo Raymundo P: Rocky Salskov CW: Pamela Mason Davey DF: NBBJ Graphic Design CL: Bellevue Club Hotel   USA   1995

119

120

1. CD, AD, D: J. J. F. G. Borrenbergs / R. Verkaart DF: Stoere Binken Design CL: Jean - Philippe Rieu Netherlands 1996

2. CD: Emine Tusavul AD: Yesim Kuscuoglu DF: T. T Reklam Hizmetleri CL: Foli Turkey 1996

1. **CD, AD, D:** Mario A. Mirelez **DF:** Mirelez / Ross Inc. **CL:** Eckert Fine Art   USA   1995

2. **AD, D:** Masami Ishibashi **P:** Akiyoshi Miyashita **DF:** Masami Ishibashi Design Inc. **CL:** Raku International   Japan   1996

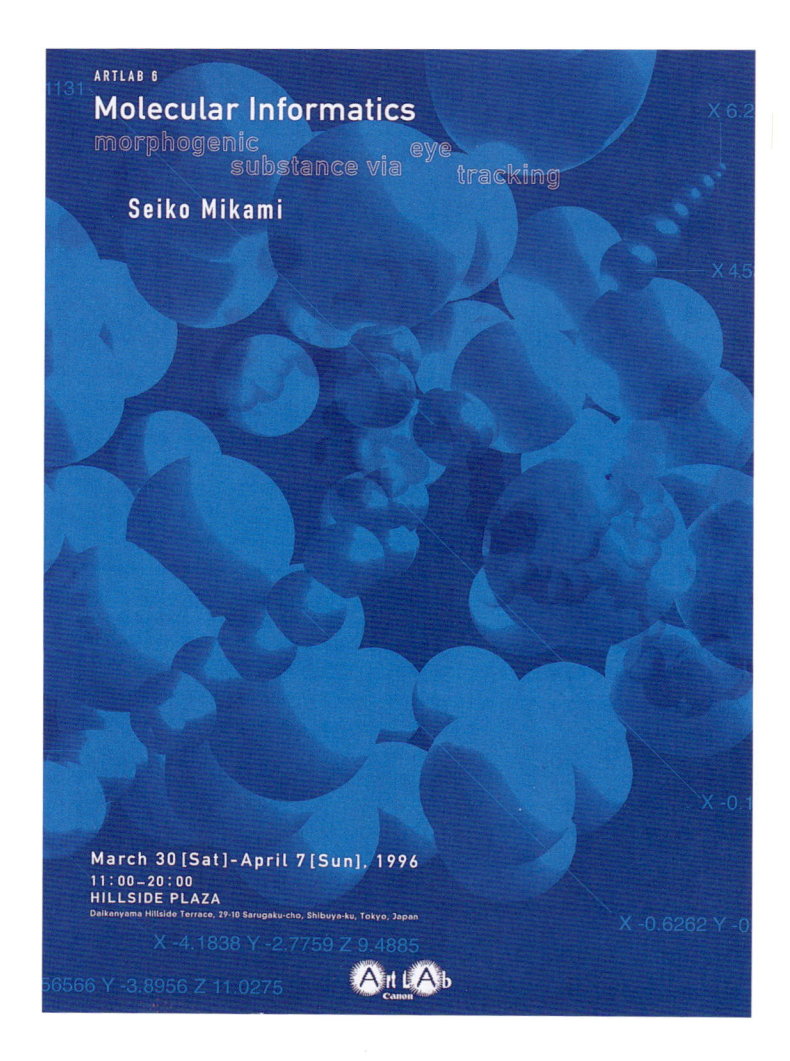

1. AD, D: Tomohiro Itami Artist: Seiko Mikami CL: Art Lab, Canon Inc. Japan 1996

2. CD: Akihiro Suzuki AD: Yasunori Arai D: Hiroyuki Yamaguchi P: Tomoharu Hirata DF: Picture Disc CL: Stance Company Japan 1992

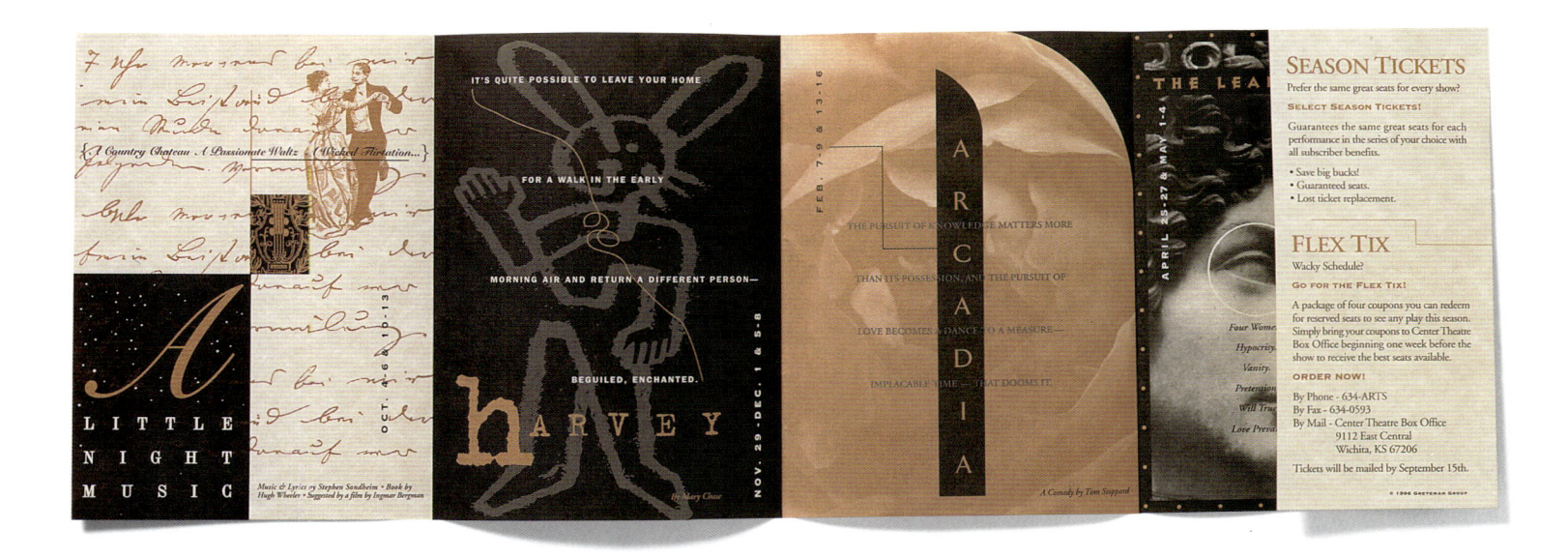

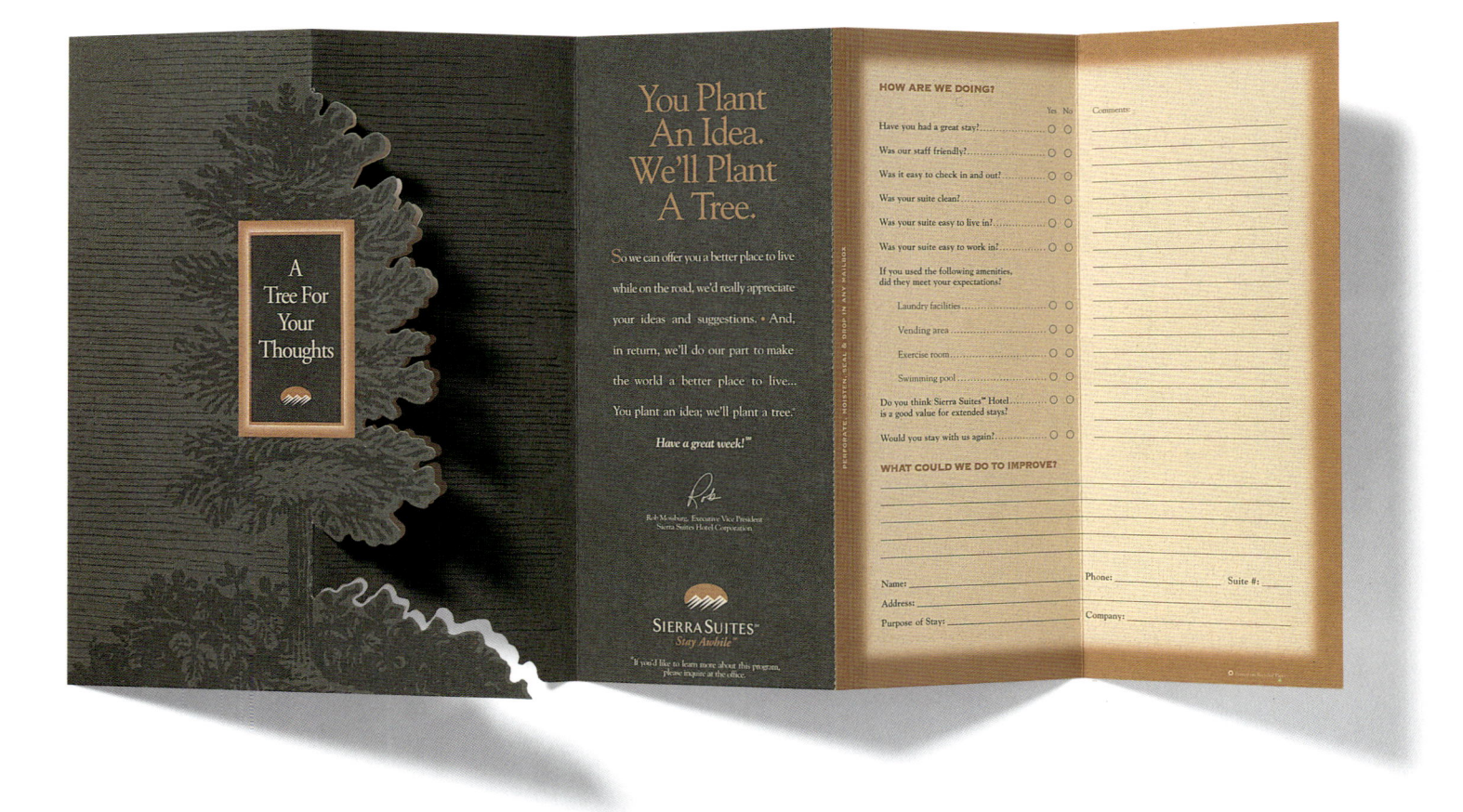

PRINTED MATERIAL

1. CD, AD, D: Sonia Greteman AD, D: James Strange CL: The Wichita Center for the Arts USA 1996

2. CD, AD, D: Sonia Greteman AD, D: Craig Thomson CL: Sierra Suites USA 1996

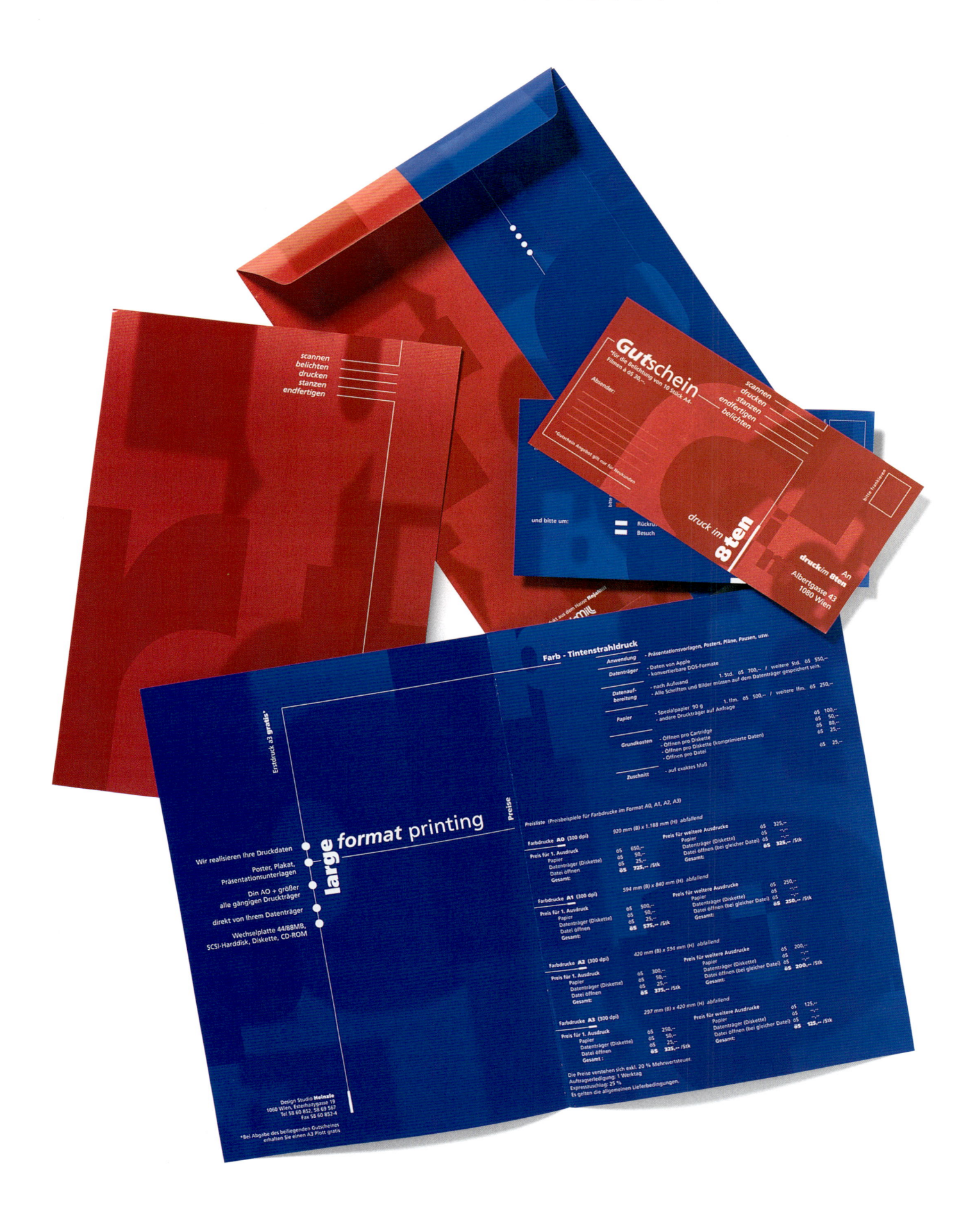

CD, AD, D, DF: Heinzle Lothar Amilian   CL: Heinzle / Druck im 8ten   Austria   1995

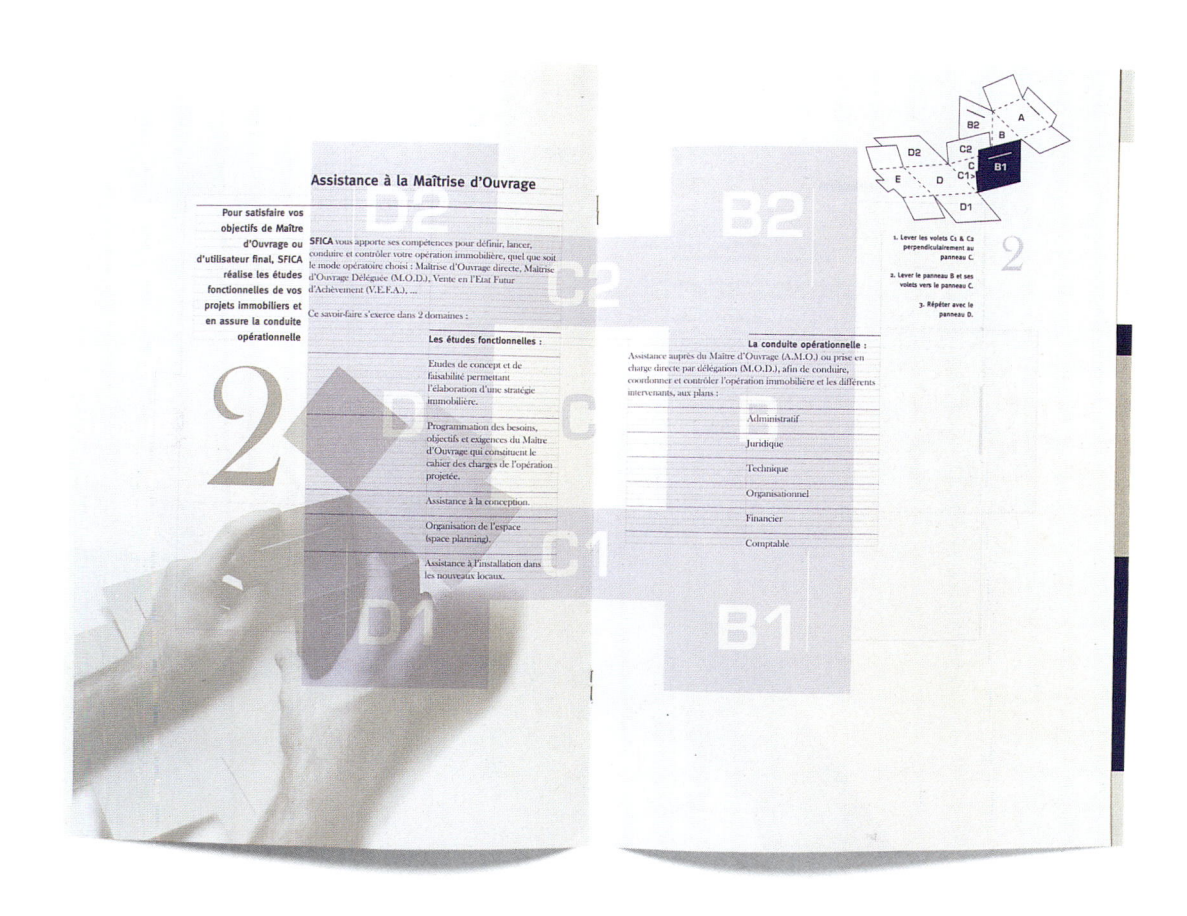

PRINTED MATERIAL

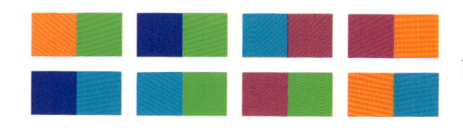

1. AD: Roslyn Eskind D: Nicola Lyon DF: Eskind Waddell CL: Avenor Inc.   Canada   1996

2. CD: Christopher Evans CL: Sfica   France   1994   *Cover constructs into a box

125

AD, D: Motoko Naruse P: Hisashi Shimizu CL: Descente, Ltd. Japan 1996

PRINTED MATERIAL

CD: Stuart I. Frolick AD, D: Darin Beaman D: Chris Haaga P: Steven A. Heller
Writers: Jenrifer Root / Geeta Sharma / Angela Rackleff DF, CL: Art Center College of Design USA 1996

127

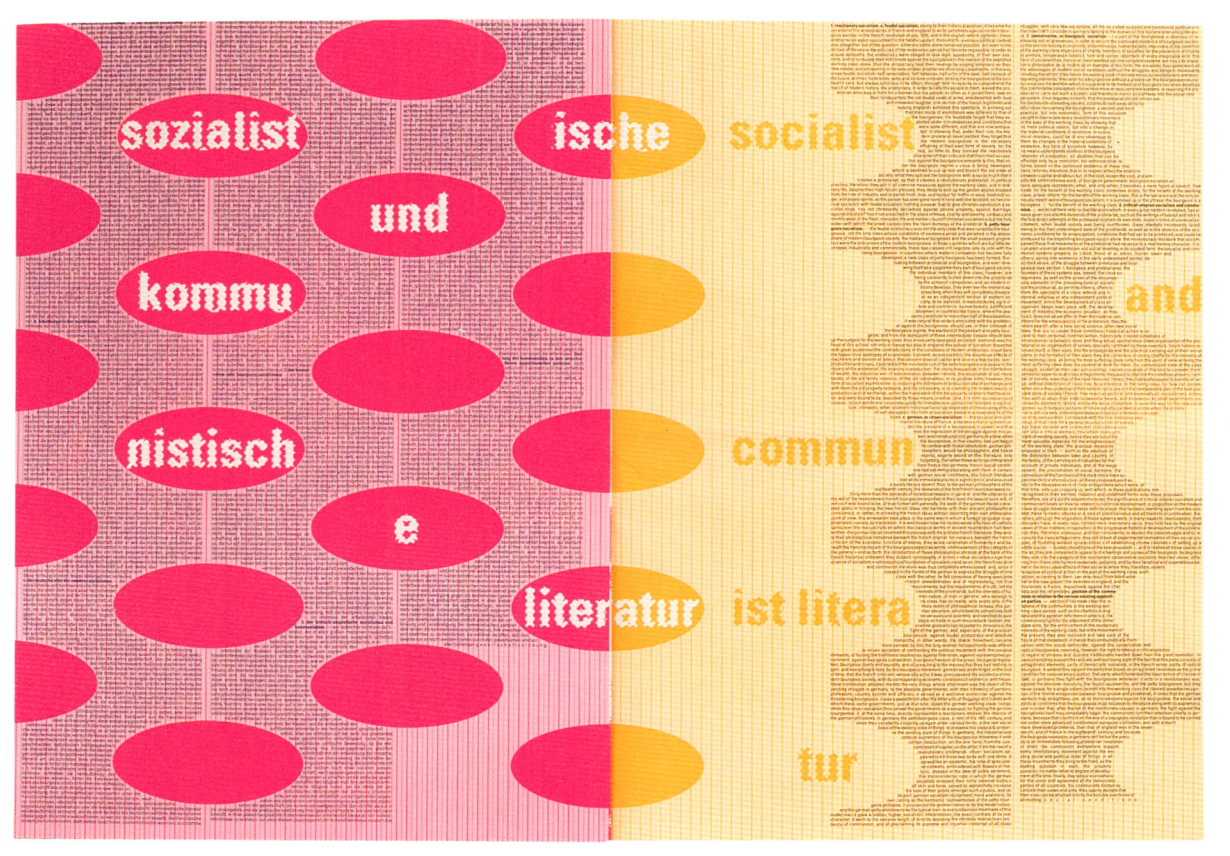

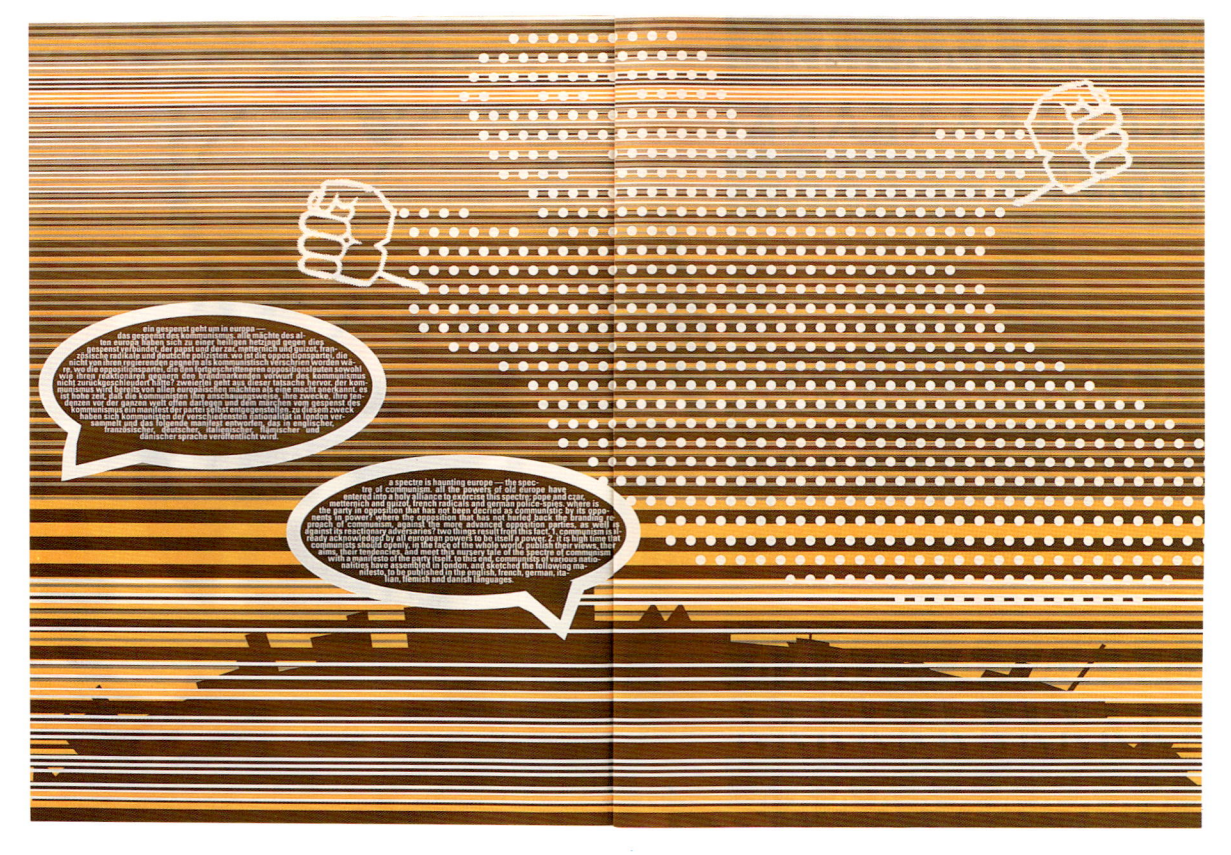

PUBLICATIONS

128

D: Detlef Fiedler D, I: Daniela Haufe DF: Cyan CL: Cyan Press Germany 1995

PUBLICATIONS

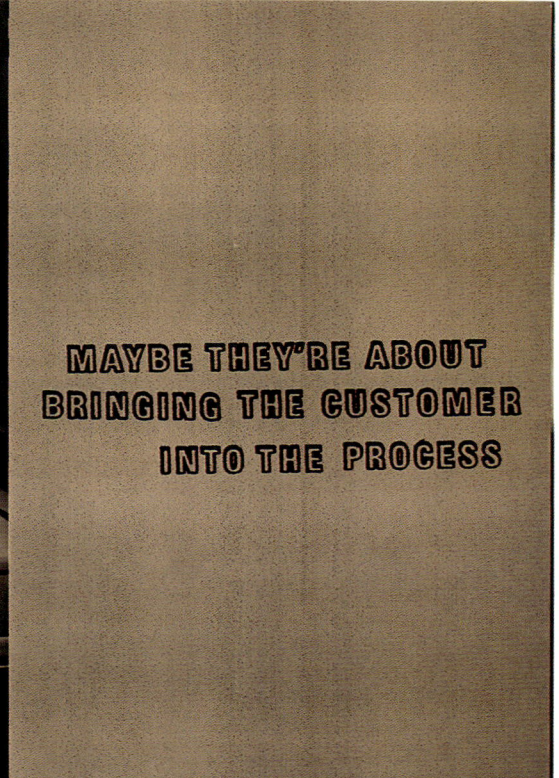

MAYBE GREAT PRODUCTS AREN'T ALWAYS PRETTY

MAYBE THEY'RE ABOUT BRINGING THE CUSTOMER INTO THE PROCESS

WHERE IS YOUR NEXT GREAT PRODUCT GOING TO COME FROM?

CD, AD: Bill Cahan D: Bob Dinetz DF: Cahan + Associates CL: GVO, Inc. USA 1996

PUBLICATIONS

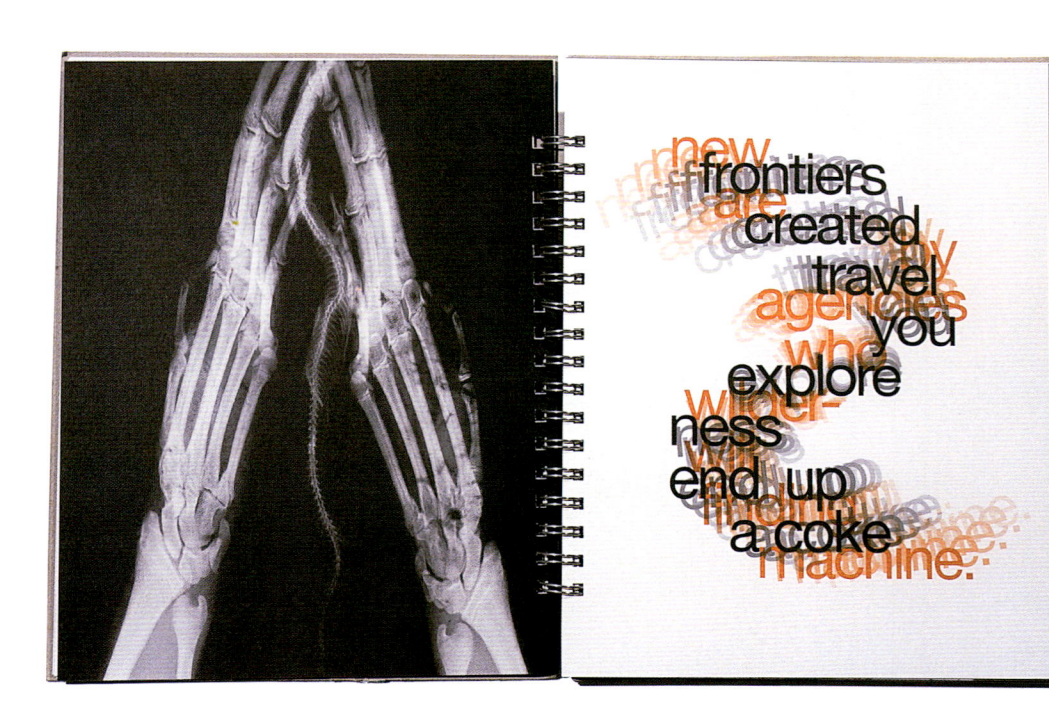

130

1. CD, D, P, I: Seán O'Mara DF, CL: Xon Corp   UK   1993

2. CD, D: Robert Bergman - Ungar AD: Giles Dunn P: Nick Knight / various DF: Bergman - Ungar Associates CL: Map Magazine USA 1996

PUBLICATIONS

CD: Stuart I. Frolick AD: Rebeca Mendez D: Darin Beaman DF, CL: Art Center College of Design   USA   1993

PUBLICATIONS

CD: Shir Yamazaki AD, D: Issay Kitagawa P: Kunihiko Takada CL: Photo Gallery International Japan 1996

133

PUBLICATIONS

1
—
2

"It's easier because I have family, but it's also hard emotionally sometimes to do things on your own. I want to know I can do it."

Taking **risks** requires courage and encouragement.

See the world in a different way.

WISB ANNUAL REPORT
WE'RE MAKIN' IT
Wichita Industries & Services For The Blind Inc.

At WISB we succeed professionally because we are encouraged to make our own choices, promoted to leadership positions, and given the authority to make key decisions. Our participation is crucial when developing policy, planning future goals, and carrying out everyday operations. Keeping the lines of communication open is a must. It isn't always easy but it is worth the effort. It wasn't too long ago that Christopher Coleman, production aide, wasn't sure he could succeed. He worked hard and soon mastered every stage of pen production. Then he started helping others any way he could. It was this initiative and demonstration of ability that promoted Christopher to production aide. At WISB, empowerment comes from within. We are the company.

"Anytime you're working for a place like this it improves your self-esteem, you feel like a first class citizen. You're making your own way rather than someone else taking care of you."

Mildred Meck, Production

E M P O W E R

134

1. CD, AD, D: Sonia Greteman AD, D: James Strange CL: WISB USA 1995

2. CD, AD, D: Sonia Greteman D: James Strange P: Mark Weins CL: WISB USA 1994

PUBLICATIONS

1. CD: Stuart I. Frolick D: Darin Beaman DF, CL: Art Center College of Design   USA   1994

2. CD, AD, D: Sonia Greteman AD, D: James Strange / Craig Thomson CL: Greteman Group   USA

135

136

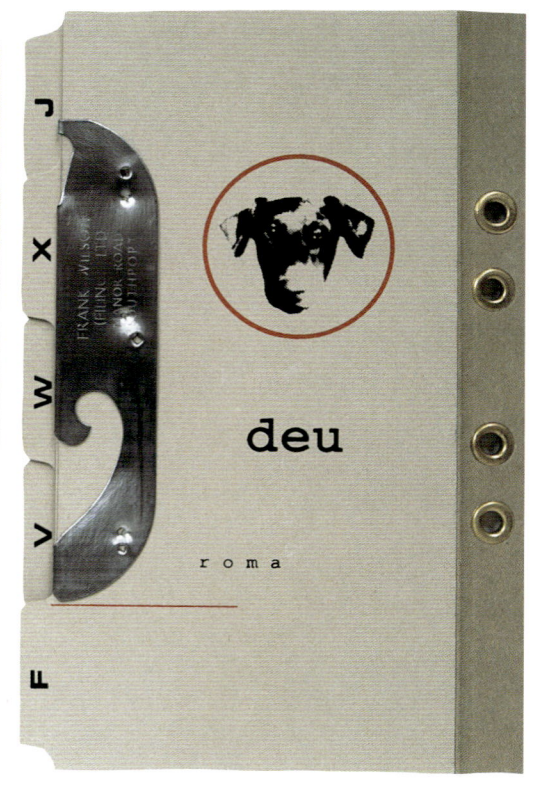

1. CD, D: Seán O'Mara DF, CL: Xon Corp UK 1993

2. CD, D, P: Seán O'Mara DF, CL: Xon Corp UK 1993

CD, D, P: Seán O'Mara DF: Xon Corp CL: Down Low UK 1996

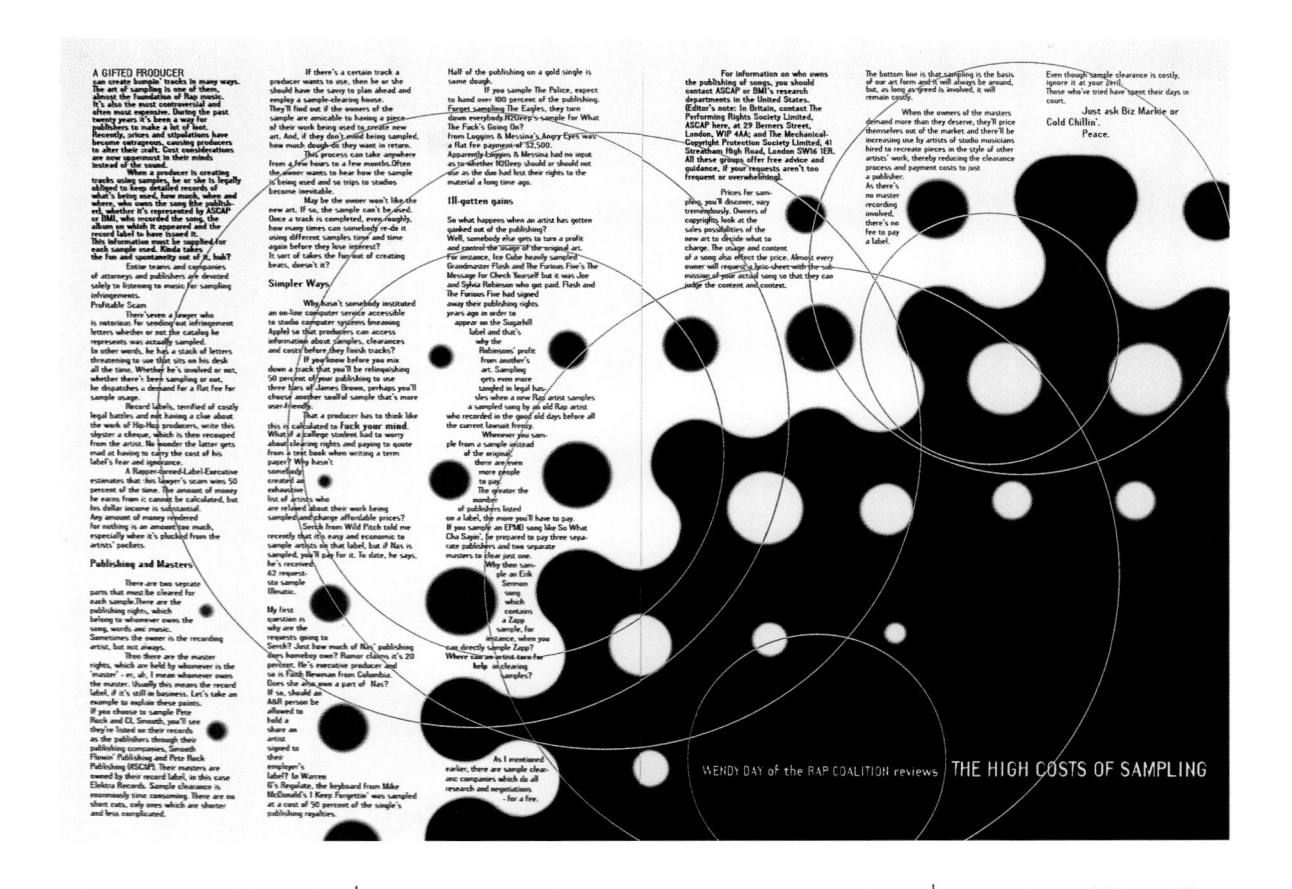

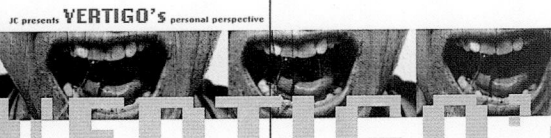

PUBLICATIONS

138

1. **CD, AD:** Lilly Tomec / Matthias Beyrow / Marion Wagner **P:** Sebastian Lemm **CL:** HDK Berlin Germany 1995

2. **CD, AD, D:** Lilly Tomec / Matthias Beyron / Marion Wagner **P:** Sebastian Lemm **CL:** HDK Berlin Germany 1994

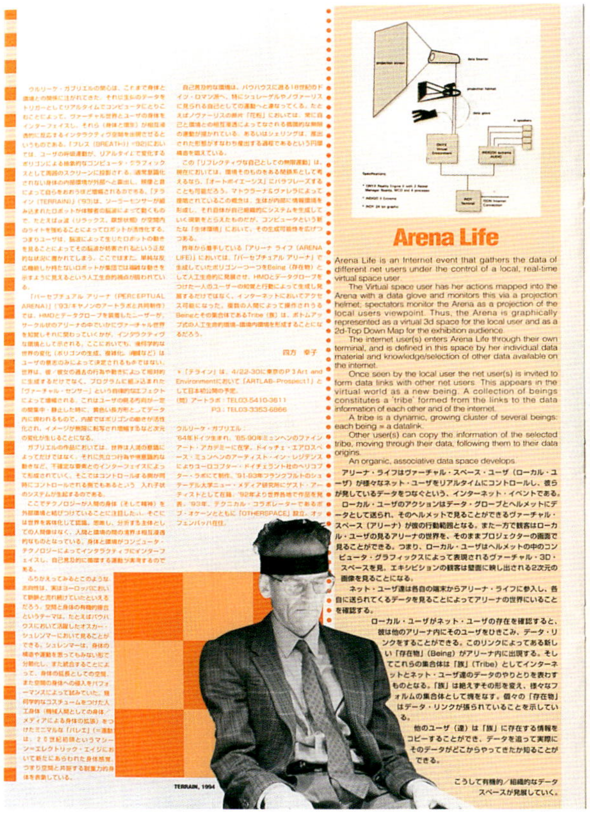

PUBLICATIONS

Arena Life

Arena Life is an Internet event that gathers the data of different net users under the control of a local, real-time virtual space user.

The Virtual space user has her actions mapped into the Arena with a data glove and monitors this via a projection helmet, spectators monitor the Arena as a projection of the local users viewpoint. Thus, the Arena is graphically represented as a virtual 3d space for the local user and as a 2d-Top Down Map for the exhibition audience.

The internet user(s) enters Arena Life through their own terminal, and is defined in this space by her individual data material and knowledge/selection of other data available on the internet.

A tribe is a dynamic, growing cluster of several beings: each being = a datalink.

Other user(s) can copy the information of the selected tribe, moving through their data, following them to their data origins.

An organic, associative data space develops.

TERRAIN, 1994

---

tech
by Timothy Blum

ION@Macworld

ION Entertainment has released some of the most critically successful CD-ROMs to date: "Headcandy" a cyber-rave "experience" with music by Brain Eno, the Residents' "Gingerbread Man", David Bowie's "Jump" and a new product to be released this summer entitled "A History of 3-D and Stereoscopy".

MacWorld, San Francisco, Saturday, January 6, 1995, post-luncheon with ION Entertainment's co-founder John Eric Greenberg and Digitalogue founder Naomi Enami of Tokyo, sitting on the steps of the George Moscone Center amidst the drizzle and throngs of confused and weary technophiles and techno-wannabes. John Eric begins waxing on his unique views about the nature of Multimedia in Japan, while succinctly rolling a perfect joint.

Jon Greenberg/ION Entertainment

JG: I love that Multimedia Japan is obviously the second most terrible development ground outside California. The trouble is what I'm seeing are there sort of not very innovative... The bulk of it is not very evocative just of energetic fusions of 50s B-side pieces of culture - the sewer forces of Japanese pop things. What I've seen is a lot of ministry. The tribe here of obscurey that I've seen from here, most of the Japanese developers should really close to help form what the medium is.

TB: What are some of the interesting things you see?

JG: I love that ALICE, the new interactive museum from Toru Marida/Toshiba [Mahjong]. There is also something called a virtual utility down—I forget the name of the developer—this is also very interesting. In general, it's a great moment for literature for the medium; unfortunately, about 90% of the product there is grim kitsch. But, I believe it's going to be one of the most important mediums, as some of the most important innovators will be made out of Japanese over there. I have a literary curiosity, Japan has been very successful in distilling culture from around the world and spit out something I see something that's their own.

I would hope that maybe MultiMedia is something that they go a step beyond and actually take a fluid rule in statement, instead of synthesizing what the rest of the world has to offer. I like the fact that Japan is one of the few places that has a real appreciation for the American culture-framed and Italian. There is more appreciation for the truly forms of media, the history of R&B or any of these things, in Japan than there is America. I think that perhaps the prosperity of Japan is keeping a lot of last elements of the golden age of American culture alive. Which is based on an interesting aesthetic relationship where because of our global economy and everything that Japan has become a kind of patron of the arts for a lot of American artists. I think this is really interesting. It again the death of the country is coming out of the present and the hard core of their parents. You've got a generation of kids who could go two directions they could go the pop-up revivalist mode or they could get out there and Get Happening some out there statements. I think that Japan is really the political and avant Gender for another Italian type culture, another era of fertility and new growth and maybe it will based in the type of new medium, not something's gonna fit Japan that's gonna unite a youth, a generation, a sort of disheartened youth, that anyway doesn't have the growth potential in their economy that their parents and older brothers were able to possess.

TB: What about as a representative of ION?

JG: I believe that ION is going to be an important player in the MultiMedia works that Japan consumes. I think there is an appreciation for innovation and that's what we are all about. And also hope that eventually we might be even able to work with some Japanese MultiMedia artist who may emerge from companies like Digitalogue or Toru Marida's Synergy or some of these other companies that are trying to cultivate art.

TB: What about projects you are working on now?

JG: I love the "3-D Zone", is our next project. It is an encyclopedic history of 3-D and Stereoscopic and I know that Japan is the world's leader in appreciation for 3-D and the viewing histories that's beyond a flat surface. They really appreciate depth and what is inherently unique about 3-D, and they are also historians of it and I think that this project will help really well with Japanese society.

JG: I also think that the project and the medium are naturally very compatible with Japanese society. So I guess this project is in a really American culture context.

Interview: Timothy Blum

日本人のセクシュアリティについて----浅田彰へのインタヴュー

Japanese Sexuality - Interview with Akira Asada

Sex

SM | **Homo** | **Porn**

What are the features of the Japanese sexual landscape at present. Two interviews with Akira Asada, the economist and philosopher based in Kyoto and Satoru Okumoto, a well-known writer, editor and publisher of hard-core pornography, provide keen insights into an arena that never ceases to stimulate and change at an ever-increasing pace.

Interview by Timothy Blum

TB: What do you mean by that?

AA: There are lots of comics in Japan and the main topic of girls' comics is love affairs between beautiful boys. This is very bizarre and in a way deeply interesting. Girls wrote these comics and sections by themselves without any regard for the real boys' life. So, there are a lot of theories. One theory goes that heterosexual relationships are too hot and too dangerous for them, so they subsidize boys homosexuality.

TB: So, in the end, boys' homosexual relationships are something that is somehow easier for them to embrace on their own terms?

AA: Sort of; it's safe stuff. And, hence the emphasis on anal penetrative intercourse. I would think that this enthusiasm about boys' homosexuality comes from girls' disappointment with heterosexual relationships. Seemingly, the girls are very free. They can do whatever they want, but ultimately there are very few job markets for them and they know that they have to get married to a silly man and become a mother and take care of a big baby (which is her husband) and real babies. So, this is a fairly dismal picture. Therefore, the only result for them is a sort of fantastic identification with beautiful boys in love with beautiful men. So, this is a very ambiguous phenomenon. On one hand, it seems that this may well be a symptom of sexual liberty at its most bizarre. But, on the other hand, it may well be a translation of girls' disappointment and frustration

with a heterosexual reality.

TB: What is the point of the frustration? Because their lives are just singularly dismal and there is not much potential for anything interesting to happen?

AA: Of course they can lead a very rich life as far as material conditions are concerned, but they know that they can't find "the real man" so to speak.

TB: What happened to the man?

AA: I don't want to sound too schematic, but I think that some ideological stereotype can be of some help. You know that they say that as soon as Japanese couples get married, the husband starts calling his wife "mama", even though it sounds a bit incestuous as far as I can see. But, anyway, the family is not so much a patriarchal pyramid as a sort of matriarchal one with the big baby "papa" and baby babies are taken care of. I am not saying that the mother is dominating. Mothers are forced to provide maternal care. Men go to school and then to work at a company etc., etc. After working hard at the company, they then go to bars and clubs where "mama" again appears as the ultimate caretaker.

TB: That would be mama meaning even the mama-san at the hostess bar or a mama-san at a sexually orientated club?

AA: Yes, they are not really, lets say, a mistress or a prostitute. As far as I can see they are caretakers, sort of maternal figures. Not always, but some of the S&M stuff and some bondage stuff etc. etc., also have elements of maternal caretaking.

TB: What about the level of

frustration on the part of the man with the witch/mother sexually speaking is there some sexual dissatisfaction with the witch/mother and therefore they are using some sort of surrogate figure? For example, I mean you're frustrated with your wife/mother and when you've finished work, you go out, get loaded and...

AA: go to clubs and sex clubs. But, again ultimately they are seeking a sort of caretaker for their sexual frustrations, so in that sense they are simply seeking a second mother or whatever. Maybe I'm talking too much.

TB: But, do both parties have responsibility for this? Is it societies' responsibility or are they both frustrated with each other or what?

AA: Ultimately, so far as its society is male-chauvinistic, I think this is the man's responsibility. But, I don't think that men can liberate both themselves and women. I think that the best solution is brought about by women. I hope that Japanese women will simply leave the family, leave their children so that children can be liberated from excessive maternal protection to go out on their own, while mothers have something to do as professionals or whatever. I don't expect Japanese men to be really independent. I would rather hope that Japanese women have more social, political and public activities, so that they can leave their family and they can leave their children.

TB: So the real change will be within the next generation - not the father/baby, but the young children that will be influenced by this departure.

AA: I think so. This phenomenon was already starting as far as I can see in the 70s and 80s. Growth became occupied by social and political activists and that was good. Children can become mothers' only and can find their own way. I don't think it's too pessimistic about it, but we are already pessimistic about this situation.

TB: What about on a different level of things, on a more expressive level. For example, perhaps Nobuyoshi Araki, his function and his relationship to censorship and maybe censorship's relationship to repression, if it indeed has any relationship. I don't know. What do you think about this issue, which has I guess over the last year really come to the foreground?

AA: Well, I'm not really sure because in Araki's case, even though his pictures are very straightforward, on the other hand Araki provides some personal content in which those pictures are somehow recuperated. In literature we have a tradition of the "I" novel where the author speaks of his own life - the death of his wife, the desperate life etc. So, Araki is in a way simply following the convention of the "I" novel - the death of his own wife etc. etc. So, even though his pictures sometimes look very straightforward and violent, the audience can understand them as parts of the "I" novel - the anarchic, but sympathetic life of the solitary photographer. So, this is a sort of literary mechanism of recuperating the straightforward images. But on the other hand, there are other photographers and other artists who are really making quite straightforward expressions and in those cases they have to face censorship.

TB: From my perspective there is a very strong thought that "My God, it's really unbelievable that we're in 1995 and in Japan" - it's a very simple story, but - "you can't show this or this or this and that leads to some other thing which may be repressed and which may lead to some strange action" - violence? - I don't know if this has to do with S&M or bondage or things like that. What do you think about this?

AA: Well, generally speaking I think that censorship and the particular legislation about the present situation. But what bothers me is a sort of implicit censorship when it comes to literature or art etc... and also this implicit mechanism of recuperating the really dangerous images and literary stuff into an understandable, human context - that's one thing. The other thing is that real censorship is not only about the expression of sexual activities, but always about the implicit relationship between sex and politics. Now I am thinking about Oe Kenzaburo's case.

TB: Can you explain this case?

AA: Recently Oe was awarded the Nobel Prize. The story goes that it started in '63 when his child was born with a huge handicap and he went to Horsensan and ended up with the literary salvation of personal tragedy through thirty years of literary work. OK that's fine. But, something happened before '63. In 1960, the chairman of the Socialist Party was assassinated by a 17 year old boy of the Right Wing. So, Oe was shocked and immediately after the assassination, he wrote a sort of story - "17" and "A Political Boy Dies" - it was published in the January issue of "Bungeijyu Kai" - the latter part in the February issue. It was a sort of psychological or almost psycho-analytical description of a young present who is less self-conscious to be on his own, but who ultimately identifies with the Right Wing and for whom the feeling of identification with the present and his army is the ultimate key to orgasm. So it's about male fantasy, which is the basis of some right wing fascist movements. So, of course the Right Wing was enraged and actually at the same time Fukazawa Shichiro wrote a grotesque parody- this was a grotesque novel called "Furyu Mudan" in which in some bizarre tiredness the decapitation of the crown prince and his wife. So both those works became scandalous and the Right Wing threatened Oe and his publisher as well as Fukazawa and his publisher and went as far as to kill

Fukazawa's publisher's maid. So it was a big scandal that was in '61. So, anyway it was a big trauma for Oe. And then in '63 he had this personal tragedy, he went to Horosmio and the rest of the story is well known. But, I think the second part of "17" - "A Political Boy Dies" - is still censored - not by legal of course, but no publisher is willing to publish it, even though he is now a Nobel Laureate. So, it's this sort of implicit relation between sexuality and politics which is really hot stuff for the Right Wing and for publishers. So, I do think that this kind of explicit censorship is still working.

TB: Do the Right Wing actually have a lot of influence? Are they actually influencing - on a very basic level again - visual censorship, in terms of the visual arts?

AA: No, this is another story. I think it is rather parents or simply conservative people. The Right Wing has some sexual complex of their own, so they are sensitive towards the works of Mishima and Oe and others.

TB: But again, there is the perception that if you cover or hide certain things then obviously there are certain psychological repercussions. If you constantly cannot directly see what's going on in a situation (whether in political or actually just sexual) do you think that this perception is true? Do you think that there are any uniquely Japanese situations that arise because of this?

AA: To a certain extent yes. Actually, Japanese pornography is much more pornographic because they cannot show the parts. So they can become really obscene without showing that parts. And of course it goes now to the various types of underground sexual activities, such as SM and bondage etc.. Again, I don't think that censorship is really the actual problem. This is a remnant of the past. They have no reason to do it today.

TB: Do you think censorship will ever be dropped?

AA: Well, it's possible, but I'm not really sure because Japanese politics is in a stalemate so no one really can change the situation.

TB: Is there one person that you think would be like, for example, if you were not you, but were a Japanese person socially "coming of age" these days. What do you think it would be like? What kinds of things are they going to confront? How would it be unique, other than if you were growing up in Alabama or a suburb of Paris? Do you think there is any unique situation or unique conditions?

AA: Well, I'm not really sure that the Japanese situation is really unique. But, no doubt they are faced with a sort of dual situation. On the imaginary level - I mean on the level of mass media imagery, or publications or video etc. - there are a lot of freedoms, everything is possible. It is a sort of paradise. But on the real level it is the old dismal situation. And also the same thing applies here, because the girls can fantasize in a very colorful way about they're sexual activities or some boys homosexuality etc. But, as far as I can see, it is a compensation of harsh reality. On the other hand, what boys are doing is to keep up with girls' expectations. So, I have that Japanese boys are really, really pretty nowadays. Maybe they are the prettiest in the world. But, it doesn't mean that they are too sexy. They are simply pretty. They are simply beautiful dolls dancing on Television. They are really beautiful, it's phenomenal. The sex has to do according to the girls expectation and the girls expectation is the compensation of their disappointment and frustration. So, it is a sort of nightmarish situation, even though it is a very colorful nightmare. So, girls are disappointed with their possible future, therefore, the last resort for them is the colorful fantasy and boys can't keep up with girls' fantasies, but that's the only way to catch girls.

TB: What about the schoolgirl thing? Not only amongst themselves, but also the use of the schoolgirl image, or the embracing of the school girl image, or even schoolgirls (for all I know) by the father-figures of Japanese society. You see it constantly in the magazines, scoolgirls, schoolgirl uniforms, even the "Buru-sera" (the panty shops, swimsuit shops, sweatsuit shops). What about this?

AA: I think this is very strange. And, of course, admittedly, it is the society who is responsible for the situation. But on the surface, I think the girls are playing the games for money or for fun. Even though adults are exploiting girls, they are sort of miserable buyers who have no other opportunity to satisfy themselves. I think it is a very complex situation. I don't think girls are victims of adults. Girls are actively playing the games, but again this is because of some frustration, deep frustration on their part. But, anyway, the fathers and the adults are simply miserable fellows and the girls despise them, but they pretend to be nice to them only for money or fun. And it's not about prostitution, its not about the real physical exploitation, so they needn't be afraid of real physical harm. Maybe it's a nice mechanism, I'm not sure. The girls are actively playing the game, even if it is the compensation of real frustration. And, I really don't know what boys are thinking about. They are simply using a lot of resources and time to become pretty to be attractive to girls.

Death

Panty

Daddy

Pink Films run in an average length of about 60 minutes, are shot in four to five days and are produced at the surprisingly low budget of exactly ¥3,500,000. Most have no artistic content; including a few sex scenes suffices to make these films commercially viable, and allows filmmakers the freedom to produce almost whatever they want. For this reason, a few outstanding films are occasionally found among them; the pornography being merely a vehicle to raise the budget for their films. Gay movies too, have derived from the world of pink cinema. Those films recently provoked strong reactions abroad and many of them are banned in Europe. At the San Francisco Gay & Lesbian film Festival '94, where many Pink Films were presented, most of the audience left the theater because of the films' explicit graphic content. "The Japanese audience are more easy going, in the words of one director, The Japanese audience usually don't have guts to flee Pink Theaters to watch these films."

CD, AD, D, I: Vision Network Co., Ltd. Japan

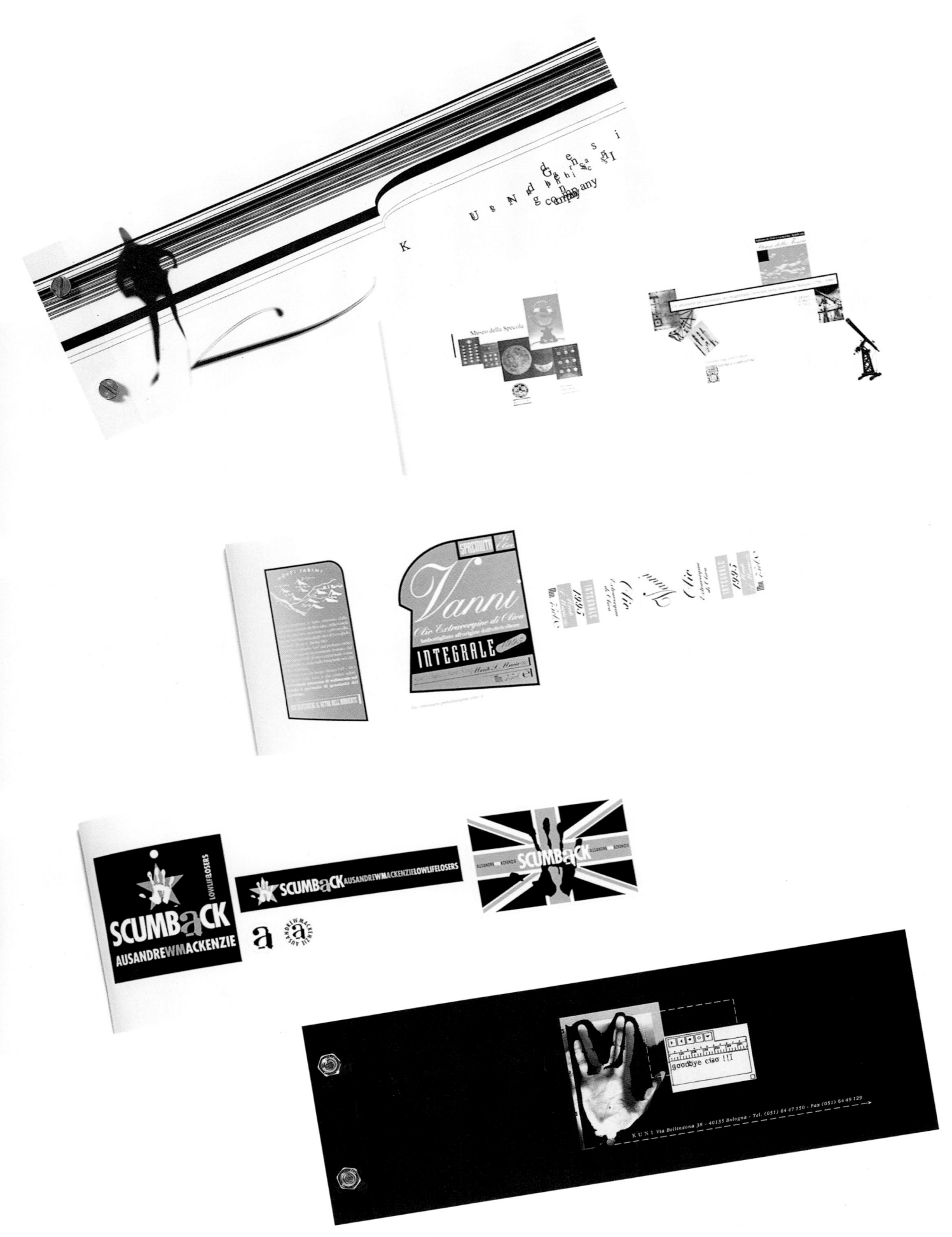

PUBLICATIONS

CD: Barbara Cuniberti AD, D: Carolyn O'Connell DF, CL: Kuni Graphic Design Company Italy 1996

PUBLICATIONS

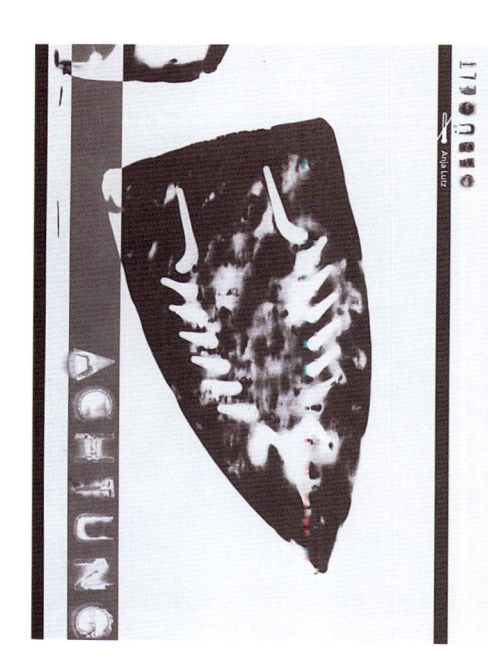

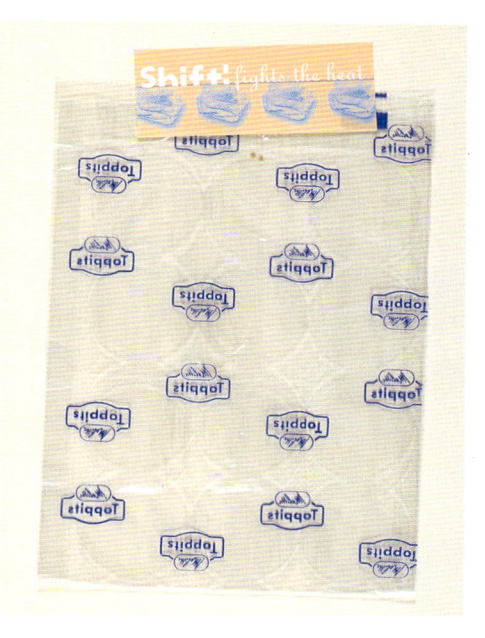

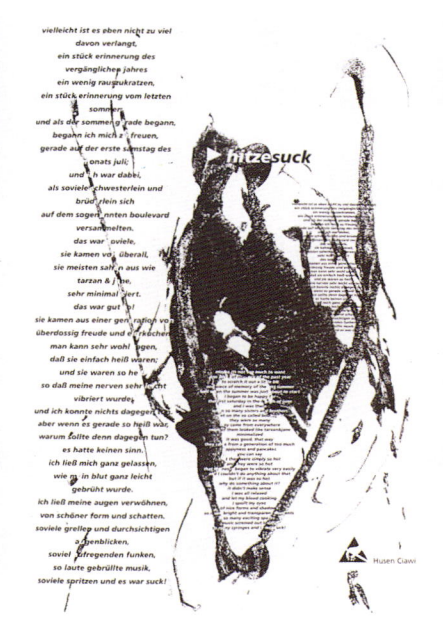

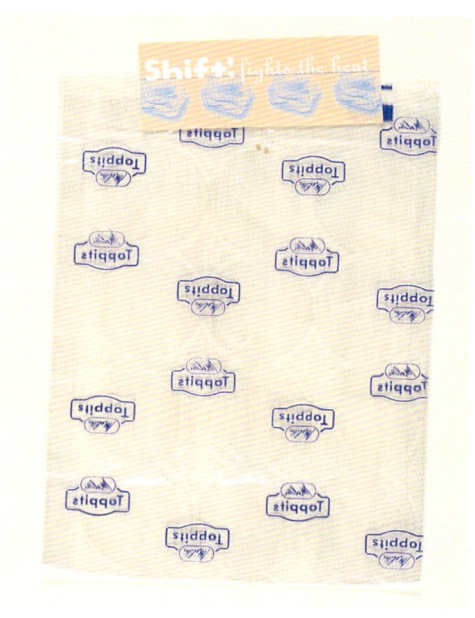

CD, AD: Lilly Tomec / Anja Lutz CL: Shift Germany 1996

141

PUBLICATIONS

TOM DIXON

I first heard Tom Dixon's name seven years ago in London. I was in a gallery and his 'Bull Chair' was being exhibited. It had a unique design and used a frying pan positioned upside down as the seat; this is something that uniquely belongs to the world of Tom Dixon. I experienced an instant affinity for Dixon's work, purchased the 'Bull', and ever since kept an eye on his development.

Earlier this year I had the opportunity to meet him in London and learned that he was interested in having an exhibition in Japan. I discovered that his recent masterpieces, including the 'S' Chair and the 'Bird Rocking Chair' have hardly been introduced to Japan, although both have been featured in almost every interior design magazine in the world. In addition to presenting his work to Japan, I wanted the E&Y Co to achieve something original – to edit and produce a special range of furniture and objects designed by Tom with Tokyo in mind.

It is my hope that the three elements of the exhibition – masterpieces produced by the Italian manufacturer Cappellini, one-off furniture and objects from Tom's SPACE workshop in London and the new E&Y production range – will demonstrate the extensive range of Tom's talent and creative energy.

Yoichi Nakamura
E&Y Co

PUBLICATIONS

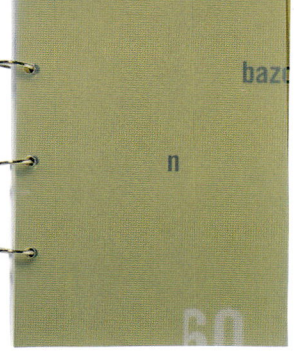

AD: Christian Boros D: Ingo Maak / Frank Müller CL: Boros Agentur Fuer Kommunikation Germany 1996

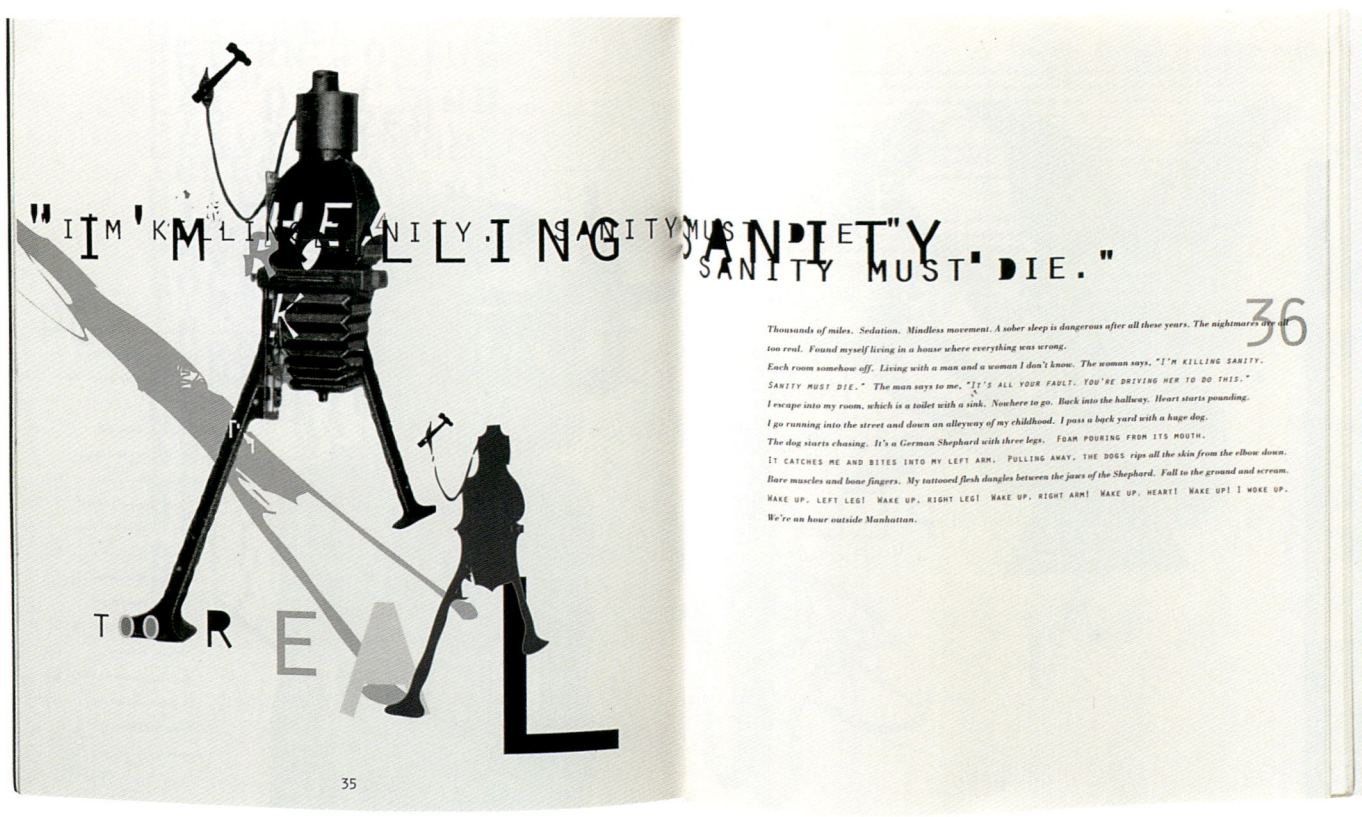

HAPPY BIRTHDAY TO ME. FIELDS. Fields of cows. Next to fields that used to have cows.

A SONG FOR THE COWS.

"BEAUTIFUL COWS. Oh how lovely and beautiful you are."

Dung of cows in the field of last year's cows. Dung buttons for tea. Dinner with lizards. A blue wrecked ship, a maraschino cherry riding a pineapple. More chi chis for my birthday. At least four more, and an endless cup of tea for neverending.

END

Dung of cows in the field of last year's cows.
END

"I'M KILLING SANITY. SANITY MUST DIE."

TOO REAL

Thousands of miles. Sedation. Mindless movement. A sober sleep is dangerous after all these years. The nightmares are all too real. Found myself living in a house where everything was wrong. Each room somehow off. Living with a man and a woman I don't know. The woman says, "I'm killing sanity. Sanity must die." The man says to me, "It's all your fault. You're driving her to do this." I escape into my room, which is a toilet with a sink. Nowhere to go. Back into the hallway. Heart starts pounding. I go running into the street and down an alleyway of my childhood. I pass a back yard with a huge dog. The dog starts chasing. It's a German Shephard with three legs. Foam pouring from its mouth. It catches me and bites into my left arm. Pulling away, the dogs rips all the skin from the elbow down. Bare muscles and bone fingers. My tattooed flesh dangles between the jaws of the Shephard. Fall to the ground and scream. Wake up, left leg! Wake up, right leg! Wake up, right arm! Wake up, heart! Wake up! I woke up. We're an hour outside Manhattan.

D, I: Daniel R. Smith **Author:** Roderick Romero DF: Command Z USA 1995

CD, AD: Koji Mizutani D: Masashi Yamashita P: Hibiki Kobayashi DF, CL: Mizutani Studio Japan 1993

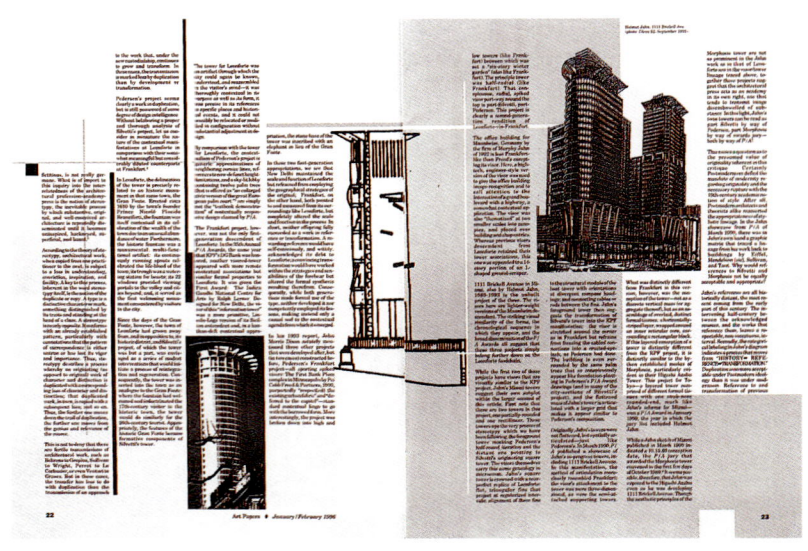

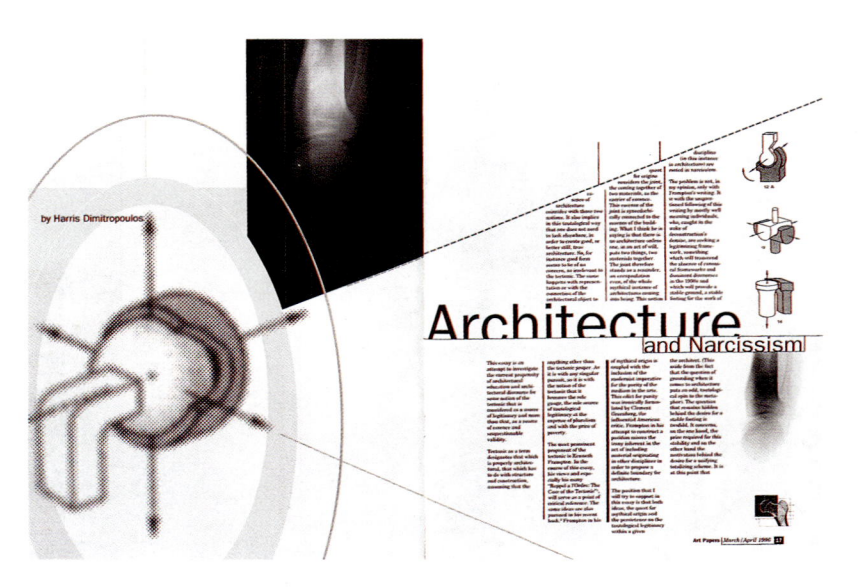

PUBLICATIONS

146 CD, D: Pattie Belle Hastings AD, D: Bjorn Akselsen D: Brock Holt / Linda Armstrong DF: Icehouse Design CL: Art Papers Magazine USA 1996

PUBLICATIONS

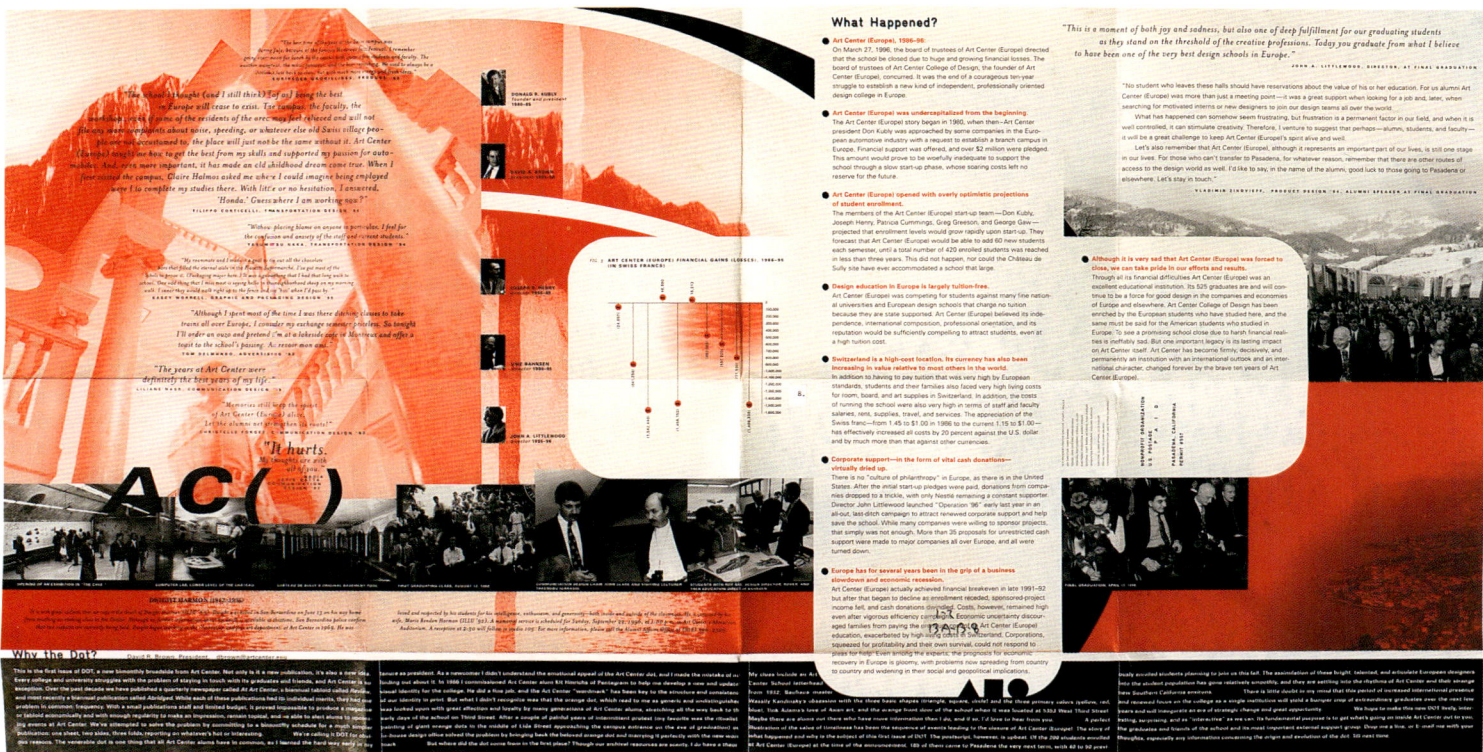

CD: Stuart I. Frolick AD, D: Darin Beaman D: John Choe P: Steven A. Heller DF, CL: Art Center College of Design USA 1996

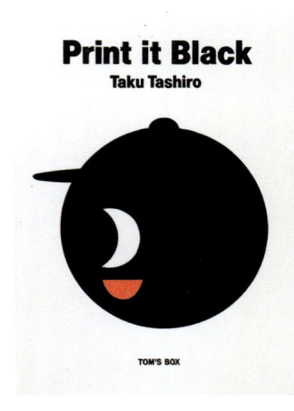

1. AD, D, I: Taku Tashiro DF: Taku Tashiro Office CL: Tom's Box Japan 1993

2. AD, D: Katsumi Komagata CL: One Stroke Co., Ltd. Japan 1995

PUBLICATIONS

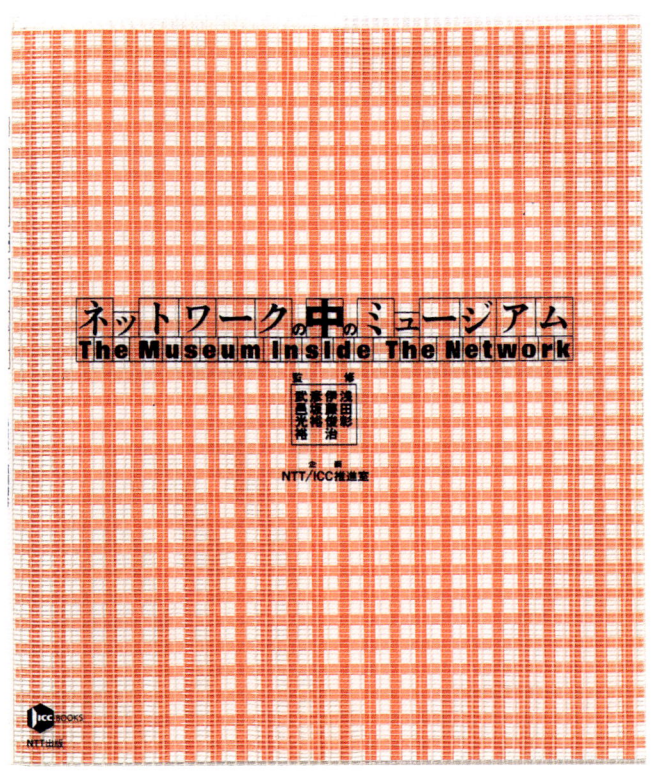

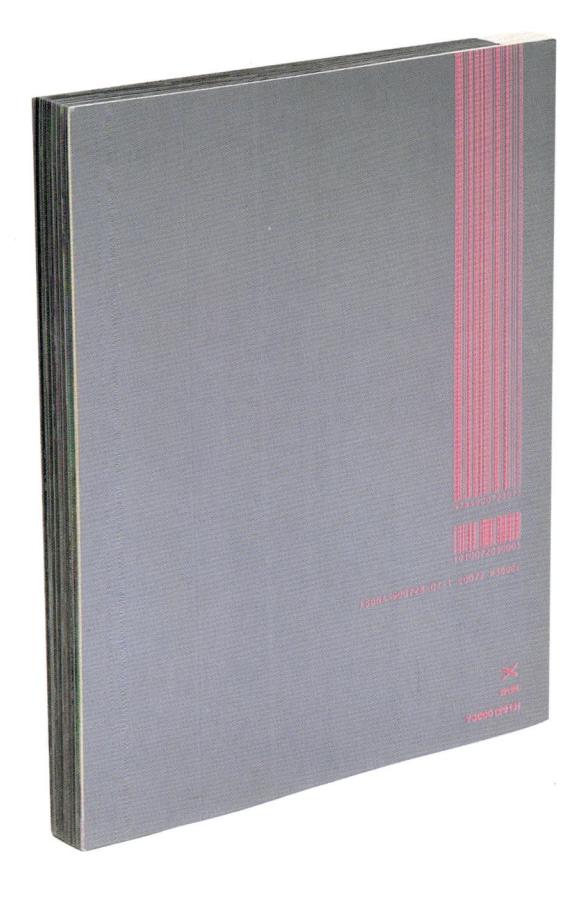

1. AD: Gento Matsumoto D: Aoi Nishiuchi / Kei Kasai CL: NTT Publishing Co., Ltd. Japan 1995

2. CD: Takashi Asai AD, D: Tomohiro Itami D: Yukio Abe CL: Uplink Japan 1996

PUBLICATIONS

150

1. CD: Curt Schreiber AD: Melissa Waters D: Ken Fox P: Midcoast Studio DF: VSA Partners, Inc. CL: Harley - Davidson Motor Co. USA 1996

2. CD, AD: Curt Schreiber AD, D: Adam Smith D: Jeff Breazeale P: James Schnepf / Ken Fox DF: VSA Partners, Inc. CL: Robert Vogele USA 1995

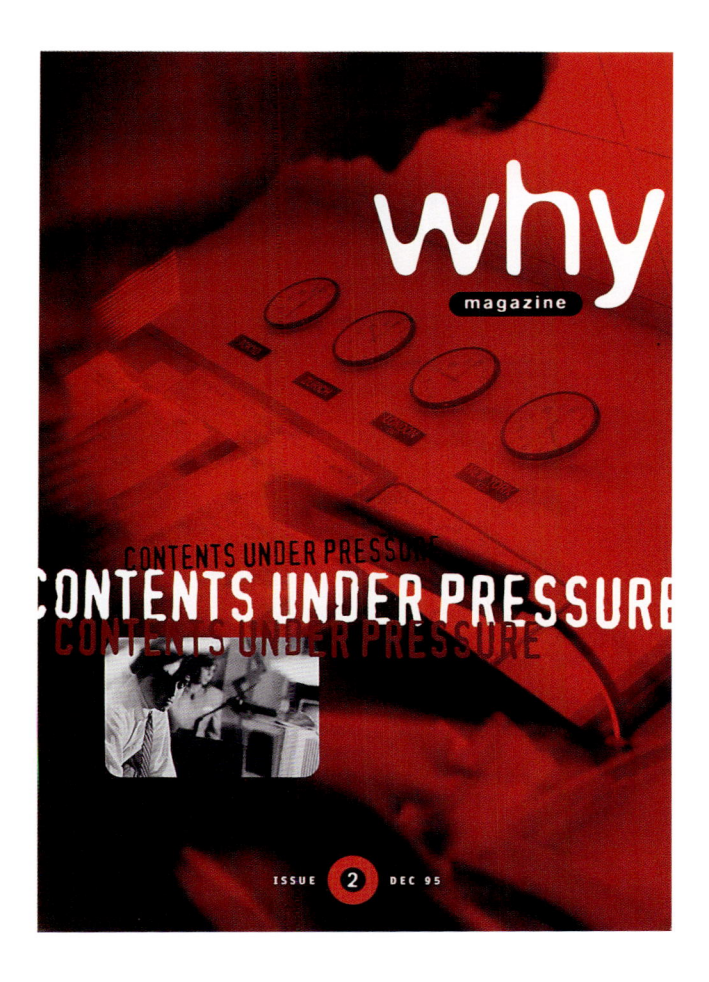

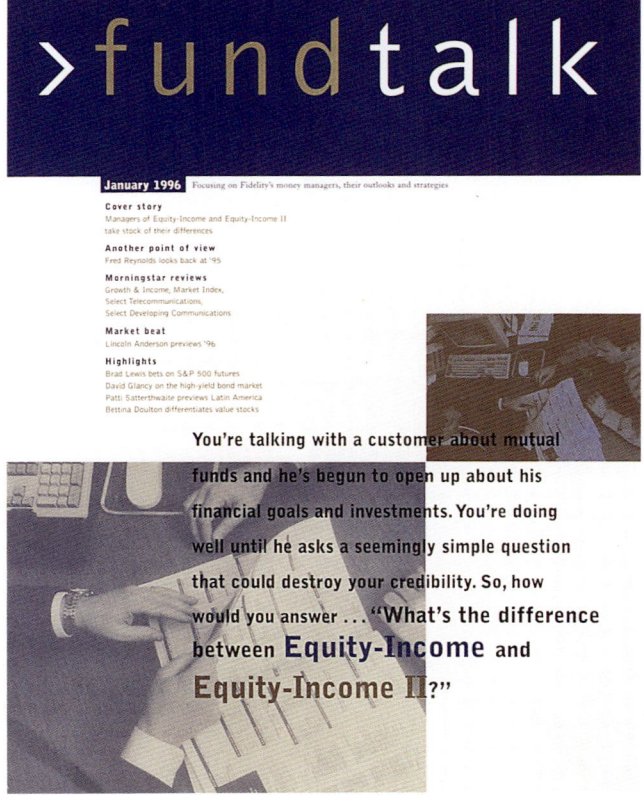

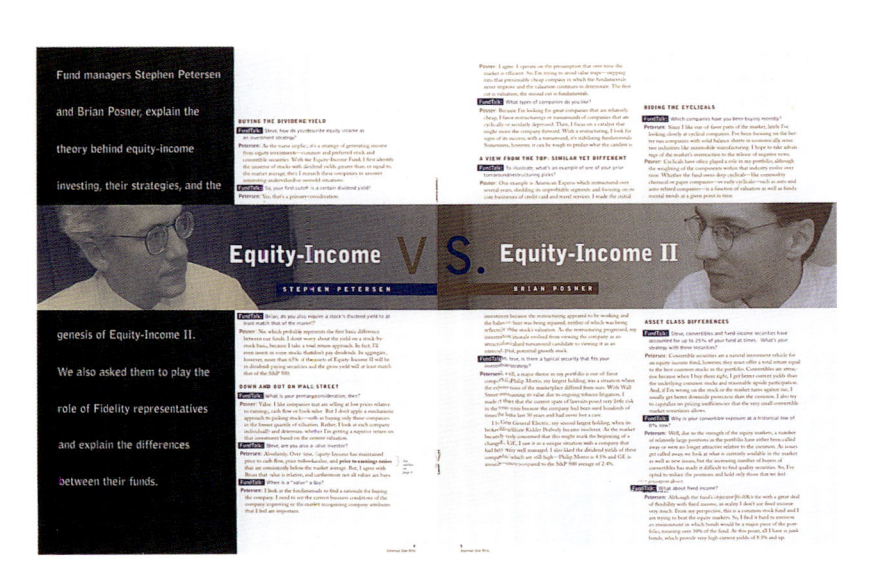

PUBLICATIONS

1. AD, D: Clifford Stoltze D: Kyong Choe / Heather Kramer / Joe Polevy P: Craig MacCormack DF: Stoltze Design CL: Fidelity Investments   USA 1995

2. AD: Clifford Stoltze D: Dina Radeka / Eric Norman / Heather Kramer / Wing Ip Ngan / Tracy Schroder / Brett Snyder DF: Stoltze Design CL: Fidelity Investments   USA 1996

151

PUBLICATIONS

152   CD: Tetsuo Fukaya   AD, D: Motoko Naruse   P: Taishi Hirokawa   CL: Shiseido Co., Ltd.   Japan   1994

1. AD, D: Koji Ise CL: Daisanshokan Japan 1992

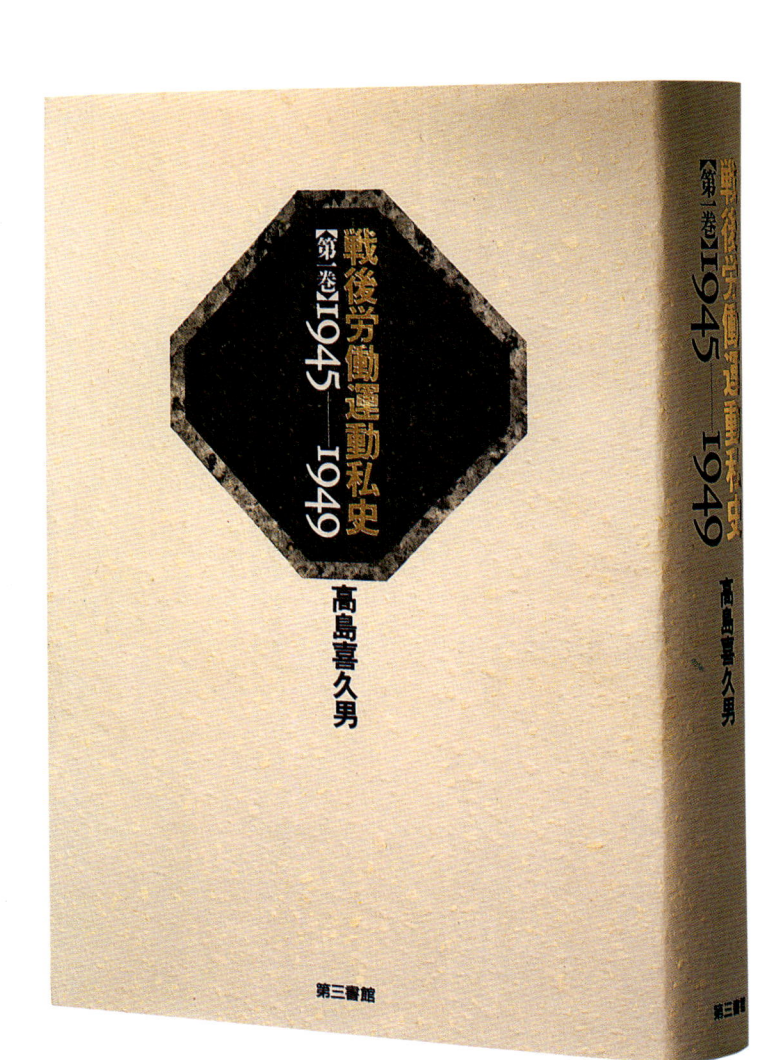

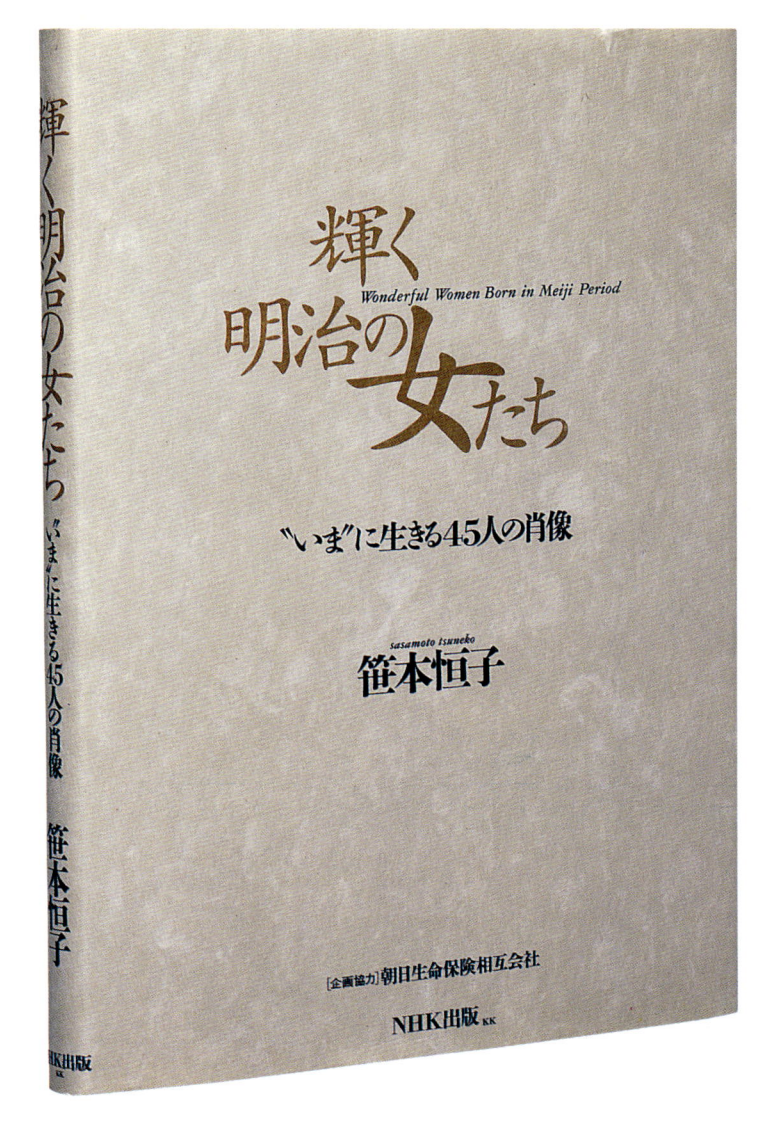

2. AD, D: Koji Ise CL: NHK Shuppan Japan 1992

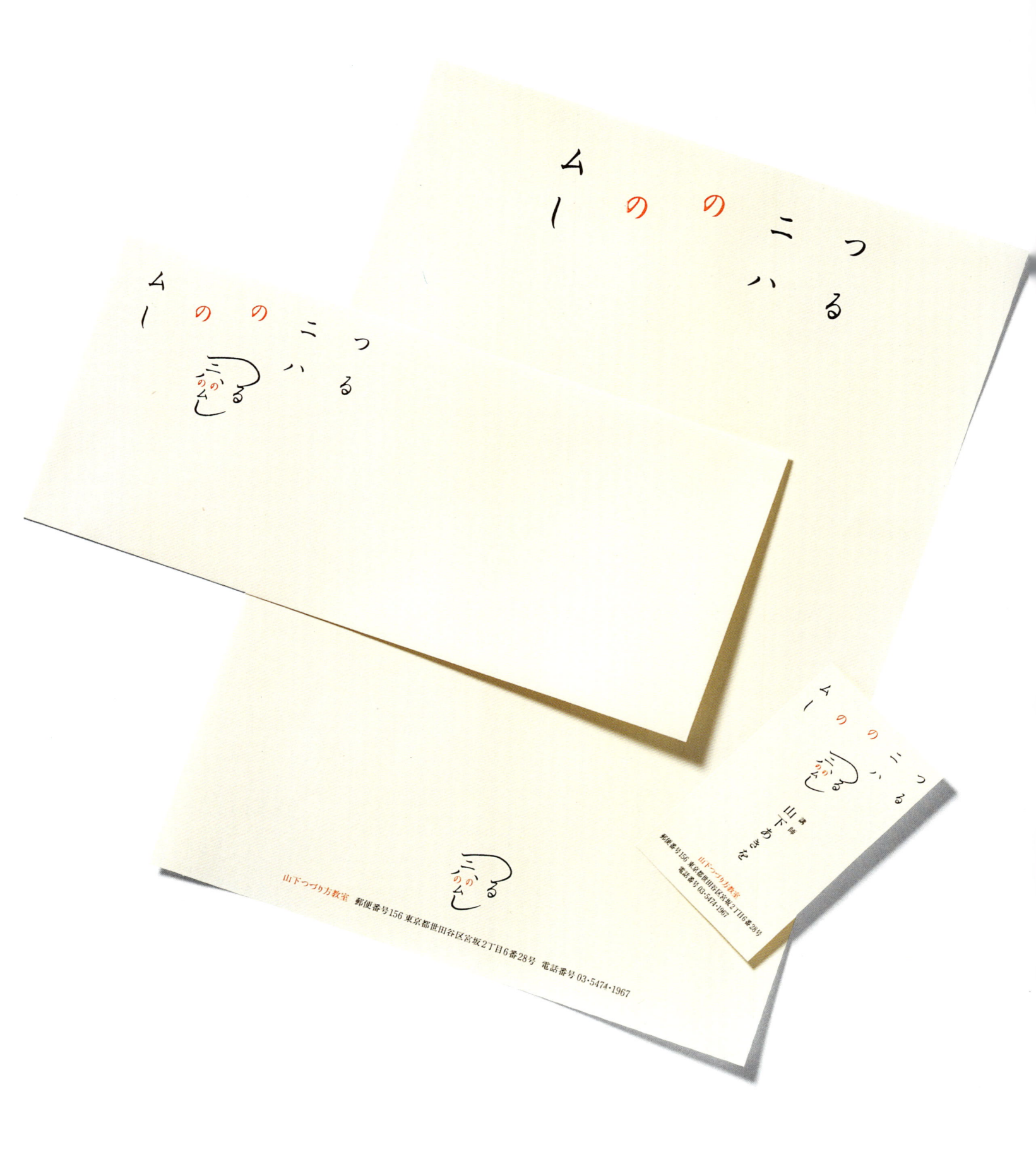

STATIONERY

D: Simon Clark P: Jason Tozer CL: Inflate   UK

STATIONERY

1, 2, 3. CD: 2. Yasuko Yoshida / Sayaka Yamaguchi 3. Hiromix AD, D, I: Gugi Akiyama
CL: 1. Gugi Akiyama 2. Sayaka Yamaguchi 3. Hiromix   Japan   1995

4. CD, AD, D, P: Rachel Miles DF, CL: Rachel Miles Design   Australia   1995

5. CD, AD, D: J. J. F. G. Borrenbergs / R. Verkaart DF: Stoere Binken Design CL: Yosh / Nash Design   Netherlands   1996

STATIONERY

1. AD, D: Marc Bastard Brunner DF: Büro Destruct CL: Diferenz Switzerland 1996

2. CD, D: Seán O'Mara DF, CL: Xon Corp UK 1993

3. D: Daniela Haufe DF, CL: Cyan Germany 1996

157

STATIONERY

STATIONERY

1. **CD, AD, D:** Issay Kitagawa **CL:** Fukunishiki Co., Ltd.   Japan 1995

2. **CD, AD, D:** Issay Kitagawa **CL:** Ajinokura Inoya   Japan 1996

STATIONERY

160

1. CD, AD, D: J. J. F. G. Borrenbergs / R. Verkaart DF: Stoere Binken Design CL: Eevo Lute Muzique   Netherlands   1995

2. CD, AD, D: Malcolm Waddell D: Maggi Cash / Nicola Lyon / Florence Ngan / Gary Mansbridge
DF: Eskind Waddell CL: Imaginex Inc.   Canada   1995

STATIONERY

1. **AD**: Rick Lambert **D**: Ben Phillips **DF**: Rick Lambert Design Consultants **CL**: Dromaius Australia   Australia 1994

2. **CD, AD, D**: Sonia Greteman **D**: James Strange / Karen Hogan **CL**: Kansas Health Foundation   USA
*Varnish

STATIONERY

AD: Kris Rodammer D: Keiko Hayashi **Printer**: Julie Holcomb Printers **DF, CL**: Corey McPherson Nash   USA

// STATIONERY

1. **AD:** Felix Abarca **D:** Matheo Clark **DF:** Abarca Group **CL:** Snap Design USA 1995

2. **CD, D:** Jim Ross **D:** Mario A. Mirelez **DF:** Mirelez / Ross Inc. **CL:** Ro-fam USA 1993

1. D: Sandy Gin DF, CL: Sandy Gin Deisgn   USA   1995

2. DF: Myriad Inc. CL: Rebecca Hansen Carrer   USA   1996

STATIONERY

CD, AD, D: J. J. F. G. Borrenbergs / R. Verkaart DF, CL: Stoere Binken Design   Netherlands   1995
*Varnish

STATIONERY

1. AD, D: Andrew Hoyne I: Angela Ho / Simone Elderi DF: Andrew Hoyne Design CL: Geo Australia

2. AD, D, I: Andrew Hoyne DF: Andrew Hoyne Design CL: Pace Event Management Australia 1995

PACKAGING

1. CD, AD, D, P: Issay Kitagawa   CL: Kasai City   Japan   1996

2. CD: Yasuhiko Sakura   CD, AD, D: Katsunori Aoki   I: Ichiro Tanida / Seijiro Kubo   DF: Sun-Ad Co., Ltd.   CL: Laforet Harajuku Co., Ltd.   Japan   1996

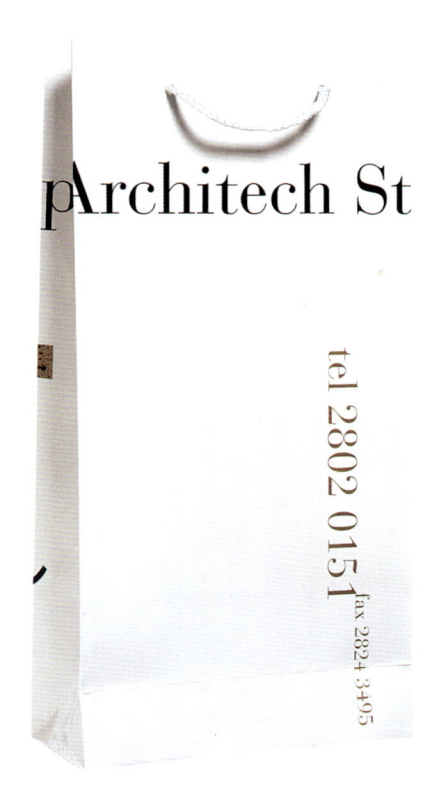

1. CD: Stephen Kavanagh AD, D: Amanda Brady P: Ruth Hurley DF: Design Factory CL: Hammet Ltd. Ireland 1996

2. CD: Alan Chan AD: Miu Choy DF: Alan Chan Design Company CL: Il Colpo / Architech Studio Hong Kong 1995

PACKAGING

1. AD, D, I(L): Motoko Naruse D: Kyoka Tsuchiya I(R): Katsu Yoshida CL: Issey Miyake Inc. Japan 1995

2. AD: Katsunori Hironaka DF: Hironaka Design Office CL: Joaquin Berao Japan Japan 1996

3. AD, D: Katsumi Komagata DF: One Stroke Co., Ltd. CL: F. D. C. Products Inc. Japan 1996

PACKAGING

PACKAGING

1. CD, AD, D: Sonia Greteman D: Chris Parks / Craig Thomson / Jo Quillen CL: Oaxaca Grill USA

2. CD: Paul Hanson CD, AD, D: James Strange I: Bill Gardner USA

PACKAGING

172

1. **CD:** Sonia Greteman / Paul Hanson **AD, D:** James Strange   USA

2. **CD, AD:** Sonia Greteman **D:** James Strange   USA

PACKAGING

1. AD, D: Taku Sato DF: Taku Satoh Design Office Inc. CL: Takara Shuzo Co., Ltd. Japan 1993

2. AD, D: Taku Sato DF: Taku Satoh Design Office Inc. CL: The Calpis Food Industry Co., Ltd. Japan 1993

PACKAGING

174

1. AD, D: Tadanori Itakura CL: Phil International Inc.   Japan

2. AD, D: Taku Sato PD: Unison Network DF: Taku Satoh Design Office Inc. CL: Takara Shuzo Co., Ltd. Japan 1992

PACKAGING

1. CD, AD, D: Leslie Chan Wing Kei DF: Leslie Chan Design Co., Ltd. CL: Shanghai Elan Cosmetics Co. Taiwan 1993

2. CD, AD, D: Leslie Chan Wing Kei DF: Leslie Chan Design Co., Ltd. CL: Nu Skin Taiwan Inc. Taiwan 1995

PACKAGING

1. AD, D: Gento Matsumoto D: Gabin Ito CL: Sanyo Shokai Ltd. Japan 1995

2. AD: Gento Matsumoto D: Kei Kasai CL: Sanyo Shokai Ltd. Japan 1995

3. AD, D: Gento Matsumoto CL: Sanyo Shokai Ltd. Japan 1995

CD, AD, D: Carlos Segura DF: Segura Inc. CL: Q101 USA 1996

1. AD: Yoshiro Kajitani D: Mayumi Kawabe DF: Kajitany Design CL: Victor Entertainment, Inc. Japan 1995

2. AD, D, I: Yoshiro Kajitani DF: Kajitany Design CL: Polydor K. K. Japan 1991

PACKAGING

1. CD, AD: Stefan Sagmeister D: Veronica Oh P: Tom Schierlitz DF: Sagmeister Inc. CL: Razor & Tie USA

2. CD, AD, I: Stefan Sagmeister D: Veronica Oh DF: Sagmeister Inc. CL: Studio SGP USA 1995

CD, AD, D, I: Carlos Segura I: Tony Klassen / Hatch / Tim Marcus DF: Segura Inc. CL: [T-26] USA 1996

PACKAGING

1. AD, D: Yasuhiro Sawada CL: Nippon Columbia Co., Ltd. Japan 1993

2. CD, AD, D: Carlos Segura P: Bettman Archives DF: Segura Inc. CL: Q101 USA 1995

OTHERS

1996

7 1 2 3 4 5 6 7 8 9 10 11 12 13 14 15 16 17 18 19 20 21 22 23 24 25 26 27 28 29 30 31
  MON TUE WED THU FRI SAT SUN MON TUE WED THU FRI SAT SUN MON TUE WED THU FRI SAT SUN MON TUE WED THU FRI SAT SUN MON TUE WED
8 1 2 3 4 5 6 7 8 9 10 11 12 13 14 15 16 17 18 19 20 21 22 23 24 25 26 27 28 29 30 31

1996

1 1 2 3 4 5 6 7 8 9 10 11 12 13 14 15 16 17 18 19 20 21 22 23 24 25 26 27 28 29 30 31
  MON TUE WED THU FRI SAT SUN MON TUE WED THU FRI SAT SUN MON TUE WED THU FRI SAT SUN MON TUE WED THU FRI SAT SUN MON TUE WED
2 1 2 3 4 5 6 7 8 9 10 11 12 13 14 15 16 17 18 19 20 21 22 23 24 25 26 27 28 29

AD, D, I: Taku Tashiro D: Masato Araki DF: Taku Tashiro Office CL: The Table Japan 1995

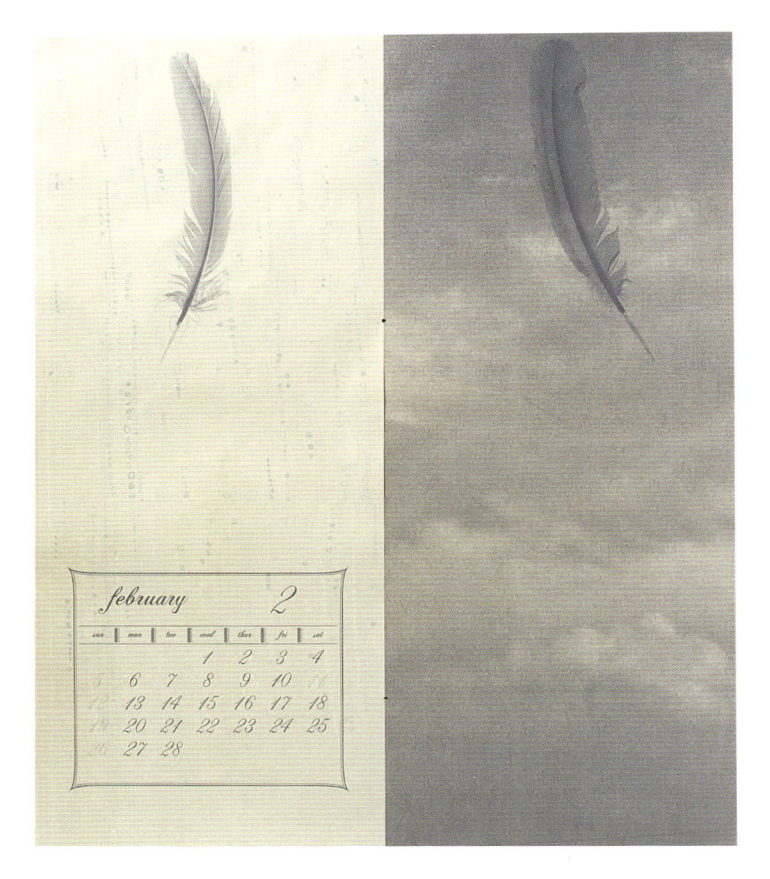

OTHERS

CD, AD, D, I: Issay Kitagawa CL: Graph Co., Ltd. Japan 1995

183

AD, D: Katsumi Komagata DF: One Stroke Co., Ltd. CL: Tokushu Paper Manufacturing Co., Ltd. Japan 1995

1. AD, D: Akira Utsumi CL: Blue Way Co., Ltd. Japan 1996

2. AD, D: Akira Utsumi CL: Blue Works Company Japan 1994

1. CD, AD, D, I: John Sayles DF: Sayles Graphic Design CL: Des Moines Park & Recreation USA 1996

2. CD: Daisuke Konno AD, D: Hiroaki Konya DF: Kokoku Nojo CL: Sanwa Bank Japan 1996

OTHERS

1. D, I: Akihiko Tsukamoto CL: Yamato Inc.   Japan 1996

2. AD: Rick Lambert D: Mike Barker / Ben Phillips DF: Rick Lambert Design Consultants CL: Dromaius Australia   Australia 1996

John Maeda Exhibition at Ginza Graphic Gallery

AD, D: John Maeda CL: Ginza Graphic Gallery USA 1996

AD: Yuichi Nakagawa D: Sachiko Kitani DF, CL: Kinema Moon Graphics   Japan   1995-1996

OTHERS

CD, AD, D, I: Vision Network Co., Ltd.   Japan

OTHERS

OTHERS

CD, AD, D: Peat Jariya AD, D: Scott Head DF, CL: Metal Studio Inc. USA 1994

193

CD, AD, D: Terry Greene P: John CW: Gay Griffin DF: Design Factory CL: Lime Street   Ireland   1996

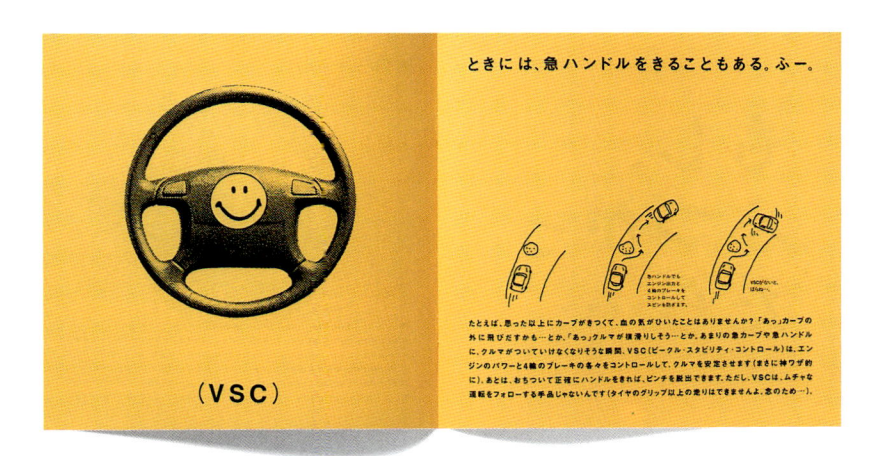

1. **AD, D**: Charles Shields **P**: Transmission Digital **DF, CL**: Shields Design USA 1996

2. **AD, D**: Charles Shields **DF, CL**: Shields Design USA 1995

3. **CD**: Hiroshi Sasaki **AD**: Koichi Sawada **D**: Takaya Shibazaki **CL**: Toyota Motor Co. Japan 1995

OTHERS

196

1. AD, D: Barbara Casadei CL: Arianova Rock Fantasy   Italy   1996

2. CD, AD: Stefan Sagmeister D: Verontca Oh DF: Sagmeister Inc. CL: Aerosmith   USA   1995

OTHERS

1. CD, AD, D, I: John Sayles CW: Wendy Lyons DF: Sayles Graphic Design CL: AIGA Wichita USA 1996

2. CD, AD, D, I: John Sayles CW: Allison Bishop DF: Sayles Graphic Design CL: Principal Residential Mortgage USA 1995

OTHERS

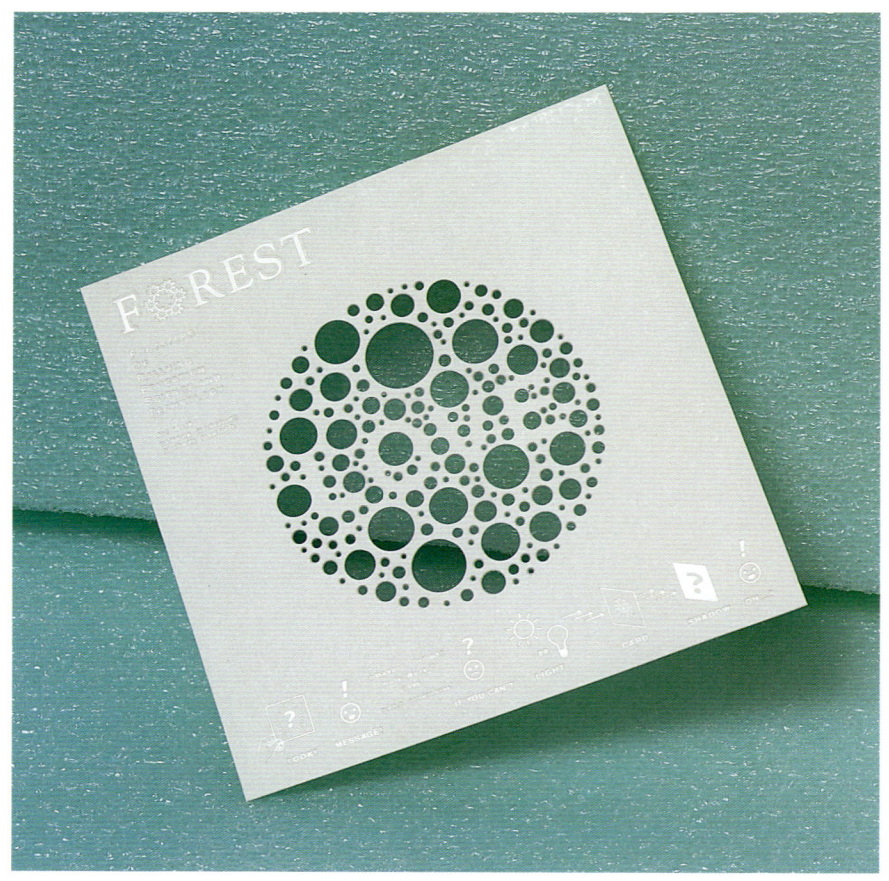

198

1. CD: Noriyuki Tanaka CD, D, Artist: Makoto Orisaki CL: Science Museum   Japan 1996   *No color
Can you see the message?　メッセージが見えますか？（Answer : P220）

2. CD: Noriyuki Tanaka CD, AD, D: Makoto Orisaki I: Yumiko Noguchi CL: Science Museum   Japan 1996
Card is inflated by blowing into it from the back.　後ろから息を吹き込むと立体的になります。

OTHERS

1. CD, D: Robert Bergman - Ungar AD: Giles Dunn DF: Bergman - Ungar Associates CL: For Life Records   USA 1996

2. D: Takao Yamashita CL: Beauty and Beast   Japan 1996

OTHERS

CD: 1. Petit Mangin / Pfaffli / Clavelly / 2. Alexandre Petit Mangin DF, CL: La Vache Noire   France   1996

OTHERS

1. CD, AD, D, I: John Sayles D: Jennifer Elliott P: Bill Nellans CW: Wendy Lyons DF: Sayles Graphic Design CL: American Heart Association   USA   1996

2. AD, D: Katsumi Komagata DF: One Stroke Co., Ltd. CL: F. D. C. Products Inc.   Japan   1996

OTHERS

OTHERS

Men's Bigi
Shoes retain original shape.
Adjustable / fits almost all sizes.
Fits shoes for pre-teen and older.
Rust proof, unbreakable.

Men's Bigi
Shoes retain original shape.
Adjustable / fits almost all sizes.
Fits shoes for pre-teen and older.
Rust proof, unbreakable.

1. **AD, D:** Akira Sumi **CL:** Men's Bigi Co., Ltd. Japan

2. **AD, D:** Akira Sumi **CL:** Men's Bigi Co., Ltd. Japan 1996

1. **AD, D:** Juliet Zeif **P:** Theo Fridlizius **CL:** Theo Fridlizius Photography USA 1996

2. **CD, AD:** Sean Perkins / Simon Browning **D, Typographer:** Mason Wells **DF:** North **CL:** Syn Production Co. UK 1996

OTHERS

1. **Ink supplier:** Toyo Ink MFG. Co., Ltd. **CL:** M. A. D.   Japan
*Recycled paper and soya ink　再生紙チップボード / ソイビーンインク（食物性インク）使用

2. **CD, AD, D, I:** Carlos Segura **DF:** Segura Inc. **CL:** [T-26]   USA   1996

OTHERS

CD, AD, D, P, I: YAT CL: Coexist Japan
*Yellow vinyl tape

OTHERS

CD, AD, D: Tom Bonauro P: Christine Alicino CL: George   USA 1993-1995

207

OTHERS

CD: Stephen Kavanagh AD, D: Amanda Brady P: Walter Pfeiffer Studio DF: Design Factory CL: Graphic Design Business Association   Ireland   1995

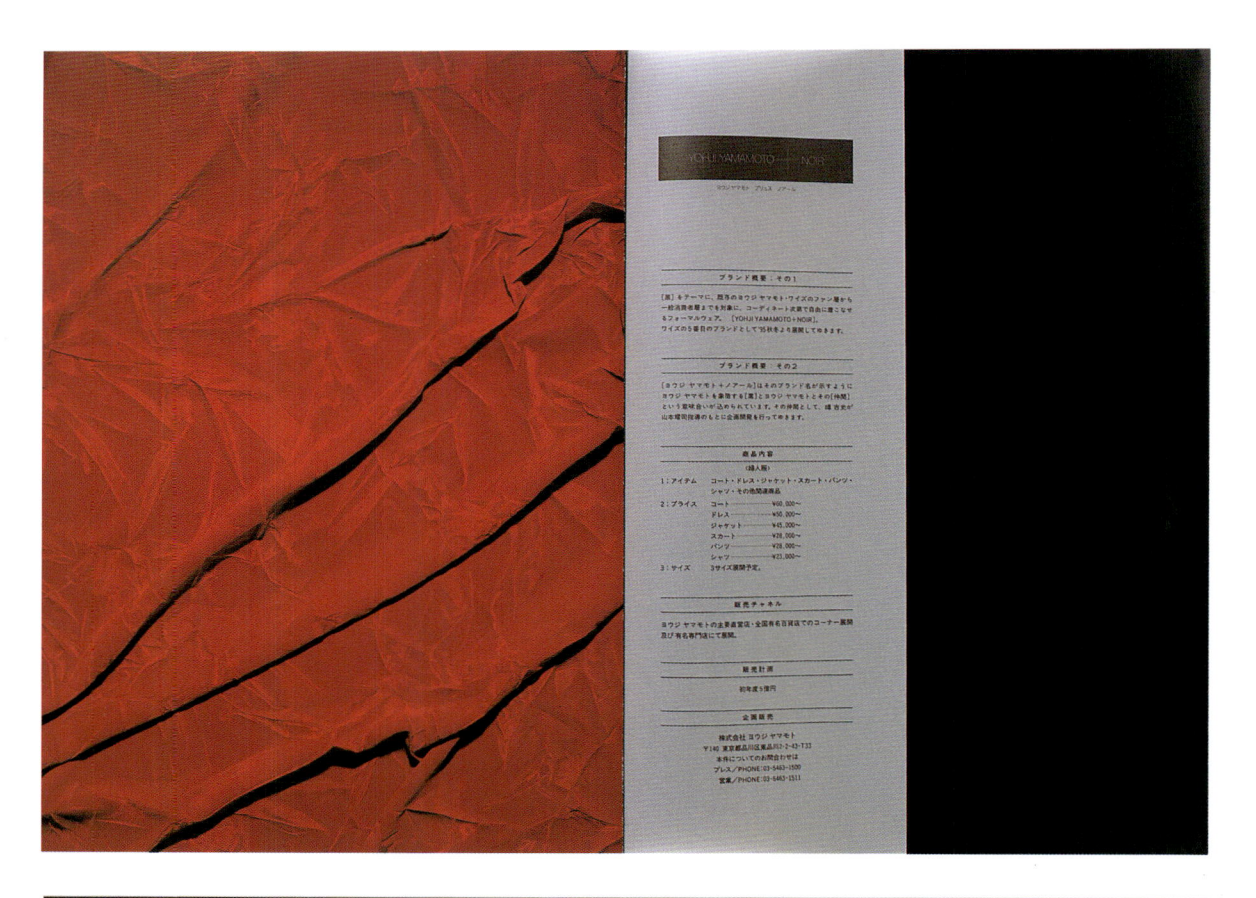

CD, AD: Katsu Asano D: Kinue Yonezawa P: Taka Kobayashi / Kazumi Kurigami DF: Asa 100 Company CL: Yohji Yamamoto Co., Ltd. Japan 1995

210

1. **AD:** Antonella Mandoli **D:** Barbara Longiardi / Giovanni Pizzigati / Massimo Arrigoni / Stefania Adani **CL:** Nike Italy   Italy   1996

2. **AD, D:** Barbara Casadei / Massimo Arrigoni **CL:** Nike Italy   Italy   1996

OTHERS

1. **CD, AD, D, I:** John Sayles **CW:** Jack Jordison **DF:** Sayles Graphic Design **CL:** James River Paper Corporation   USA   1995

2. **CD:** Emine Tusavul **AD:** Faruk Baydar **DF:** T. T Reklam Hizmetleri **CL:** Limon Co.   Turkey   1995

OTHERS

CD, AD, D, CL: Alto Campo Company   Japan

OTHERS

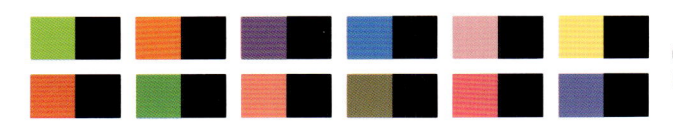

CD, AD: Sayuri Takahata D: Kaoru Matsui / Noriko Kubo
I: T. Sarry CL: Mycal Honmoku Japan 1992-1995

CD, AD, D: Hidenori Okahashi DF: Lotoath Deisgn Studio CL: Pros. Japan 1996

OTHERS

AD, D: Katsunori Hironaka DF: Hironaka Design Office CL: K. Corporation Japan 1993

1. AD: Charles Shields D: Juan Vega / Laura Thornton DF: Shields Design CL: Valliwide Bank   USA   1993

2. AD, D: Katsunori Hironaka DF: Hironaka Design Office CL: Murata Clinic   Japan   1993

index of submittors

japanese submittors

㈱アーサー・ハンドレッド・カンパニー 209
㈱アイム 17, 158
アウトノミア グラフィックデプト 99
青木克憲 24, 25, 54, 102, 167
秋山具義 15, 54, 73, 106, 156
アップリンク 149
㈱アルトカンポ カンパニー 212, 213
アンテナグラフィック ベース 97, 203
㈲石橋政美デザイン室 121
㈱イズタニケンゾウ事務所 107
伊勢功治 153
板倉忠則 174
㈱イッセイ ミヤケ 59
イット イズ デザイン 122
伊藤桂司 22, 80, 81
イメージフォーラム 72
ヴィジョンネットワーク 139, 190, 191
内海 彰 109, 185
㈱エイネット 59
岡 記生 16
奥村昭夫 27
大人計画 86, 92
オフィス サンドスケイプ 80, 81, 110, 111
織咲 誠 60, 198
梶谷デザイン 178
菊池 靖 98
キネマムーン グラフィックス 71, 189
木村悦子 57, 96
木村経典 49
工藤規雄 49
椚田 透 87
クラブ カバー 73
グラフ㈱ 95, 102, 133, 159, 167, 183
コーイグジスト 206
㈲広告農場 89, 93, 186
ゴーゴー プロジェクト 88, 103
佐古田英一 53, 89, 93
佐藤晃一 21
㈱佐藤卓デザイン事務所 173, 174
㈱サルブルネイ 149, 176
沢田耕一 195
澤田泰廣デザイン室 84, 181
㈱三協エージェンシー 41
ザ・ルーム 66
シネマ キャッツ 58, 116
ジーワークス 97
スタンス・カンパニー 86, 122
スペースラボ イエロー 71, 104
㈱ソニー ミュージックエンタテインメント 40
㈲滝内デザイン事務所 98, 101
竹智こずえ 26
田代 卓事務所 148, 182
塚本明彦 図案倶楽部 154, 187
津村正二 86
ツモリチサト 58
デザイナトリウム 100
㈱デュアル グローイング システム 99
㈱東京キャン 73, 103
友枝雄策 20
ナイロン100℃/㈱シリーウォーク 87
中村至男 23, 49, 103
永井正己 192, 205
成瀬始子 126, 152, 169
ニーハイメディア 38

㈱ニコル 61, 85
㈱パッケージング ディレクション 170
平野敬子事務所 52
㈲弘中デザイン事務所 169, 215, 216
ビューティ：ビースト 68, 199
福島 治 14
ポジトロン 104
水谷事務所 145
村松博紀 105
モス デザインユニット 70, 87, 95
横尾忠則 10
リズミック ガーデン 66
ロトアス デザインスタジオ 214
ワンストローク 91, 148, 169, 184, 201

all submittors

A-net Inc. 59
Abarca Group 163
Active White Space 67
Akihiko Tsukamoto Design Club 154, 187
Akio Okumura 27
Akira Utsumi 109, 185
Alan Chan Design Company 168
Alto Campo Company 212, 213
AND (Trafic Grafic) 18, 19
Andrew Hoyne Design 74, 166
Antenna Graphic Base 97, 203
Art Center College of Design - Design Office 75, 78, 112, 114, 127, 132, 135, 147
Asa 100 Company 209
Atelier Tadeusz Piechura 48
Autonomia Graphic Dept. 99

Beauty : Beast 68, 199
Bergman-Ungar Associates 130, 131, 199
Bleu Élastique 35, 80, 81
Boros Agentur Fuer Kommunikation 143
Büro Destruct 69, 70, 71, 157

Cahan + Associates 129
Case 51, 63
Cato & Berro Diseño 108
Chisato Tsumori 58
Cinema Cats 58, 116
Club Cover 73
Coexist 206
Command Z 43, 144
Corey McPherson Nash 162
Cyan 10, 11, 28, 29, 30, 31, 32, 33, 128, 157

David Calderley 69
Design Factory 168, 194, 208
Designatorium 100
Dual Growing System Inc. 99

Eiichi Sakota 53, 89, 93
Emanuel Barbosa Design 36
Eskind Waddell 125, 160
Etsuko Kimura 57, 96
Evansandwong 125

Fly 142

G-Works 97
George 207

Go-Go Project 88, 103
Graph Co., Ltd. 95, 102, 133, 159, 167, 183
Grappa Design 46, 47
Greteman Group 37, 42, 77, 113, 123, 134, 135, 161, 171, 172
Grundy & Northedge 88
Gugi Akiyama 15, 54, 73, 106, 156

Heinzle Lothar Amilian 124
Hiroki Muramatsu 105
Hironaka Design Office 169, 215, 216
Hornall Anderson Design Works 77

I'm Co., Ltd. 17, 158
Icehouse Design 42, 146
Image Forum 72
Inflate 155, 202
Interface Designers 36, 107
Isabelle Dervaux 90
Issey Miyake Inc. 59
It Is Design 122

J. Graham Hanson Design 52
John Maeda 188
Julie Holcomb Printers 162

Kajitany Design 178
Kari Piippo oy 53
Katsu Kimura & Packaging Direction Co., Ltd. 170
Katsunori Aoki 24, 25, 54, 102, 167
Keiji Ito 22, 80, 81
Keiko Hirano Studio 52
Keisuke Kimura 49
Kenzo Izutani Office Corporation 107
Kinema Moon Graphics 71, 189
Kinetik Communication Graphics, Inc. 116
Kisei Oka 16
Knee High Media 38
Koichi Sato 21
Koichi Sawada 195
Koji Ise 153
Kokoku Nojyo 89, 93, 186
Kozue Takechi 26
Kuni Graphic Design Company 140

La Vache Noire 200
Leslie Chan Design Co., Ltd. 112, 175
Lilly Tomec 138, 141
Lotoath Design Studio 214

Makoto Orisaki 60, 198
Masami Ishibashi Design Inc. 121
Masami Nagai 192, 205
Matite Giovanotte 196, 210
Metal Studio Inc. 193
Michel Bouvet 43, 53
Mirelez / Ross Inc. 94, 113, 121, 163
Mizutani Studio 145
Modern Dog 83
"Moss" Design Unit 70, 87, 95
Motoko Naruse 126, 152, 169
Myriad Inc. 79, 164

NBBJ Graphic Design 78, 110, 111, 119
Nicole Co., Ltd. 61, 85
Norio Kudo 49
Norio Nakamura 23, 49, 103
North 204

Nylon 100°C / Silly Walk Co., Ltd. 87

Office Sandscape 80, 81, 110, 111
One Stroke Co., Ltd. 91, 148, 169, 184, 201
Osamu Fukushima 14
Otona Keikaku 86, 92

Pandora's Box 56
Poagi® 76
Positron 104
Prototype Design 62

Rachel Miles Design 156
Ralph Schraivogel 45
Retarded Whore Productions 72
Rhythmic Garden 66
Rick Lambert Design Consultants 161, 187

Sagmeister Inc. 44, 45, 117, 179, 196
Sandy Gin Design 72, 164
Sankyo Agency Co., Ltd. 41
Saru Burunei Co., Ltd. 149, 176
Sayles Graphic Design 39, 55, 186, 197, 201, 211
Segura Inc. 39, 82, 177, 180, 181, 205
Shannon Beer 114, 118
Shields Design 101, 195, 216
Shoji Tsumura 86
Simon Sernec 107
Sony Music Entertainment (Japan) Inc. 40
Space Lab Yellow 71, 104
Stance Company 86, 122
Steven Brower Design 50
Stoere Binken Design 99, 120, 156, 160, 165
Stoltze Design 84, 115, 151

Tadanori Itakura 174
Tadanori Yokoo 10
Takiuchi Design Office 98, 101
Taku Satoh Design Office Inc. 173, 174
Taku Tashiro Office 148, 182
The Apollo Program 34
The Design Company 66
The Design Foundry 115
The Design Group 117
The Riordon Design Group Inc. 82, 118
The Room 66
The Weller Institute for the Cure of Design, Inc. 37
Theo Fridlizius Photography 204
Tokyo Can Co., Ltd. 73, 103
Toru Kunugida 87
Trouble 64, 65
T.T Reklam Hizmetleri 120, 211

U-cef Hanjani 12
Uplink 149

Van Den Beginne bv 67
Vision Network Co., Ltd. 139, 190, 191
Voice Design 100
VSA Partners 40, 41, 150

Xon Corp 13, 130, 131, 136, 137, 157

Yasuhiro Sawada Design Studio 84, 181
Yasushi Kikuchi 98
Yusaku Tomoeda 20

Art Direction & Design
Douglas Gordon

Editor
Tomoe Nakazawa

Photographer
Kuniharu Fujimoto

Coordinator
Naoko Arai

English Translator
Sue Herbert

Typesetter
Yutaka Hasegawa

Publisher
Shingo Miyoshi

one & two color graphics
1＆2色グラフィックス

1997年 3月 18日 初版第 1刷発行

定価16,000円（本体15,534円）

発行所　ピエ・ブックス
〒170 東京都豊島区駒込4-14-6-301
Tel:03-3940-8302 Fax:03-3576-7361
e-mail: piebooks@bekkoame.or.jp

©1997 P・I・E Books

Printed in Hong Kong

本書の収録内容の無断転載、複写、引用等を禁じます。
落丁・乱丁はお取り替え致します。

ISBN4-89444-040-7 C3070 P16000E

Answer: LOVE

THE P·I·E COLLECTION

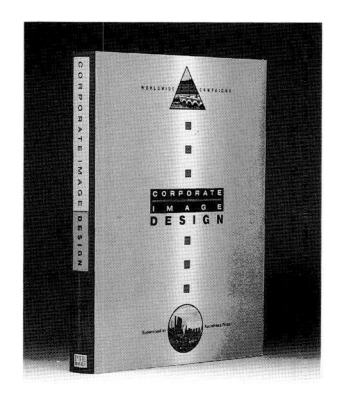

CORPORATE IMAGE DESIGN
世界の業種別CI・ロゴマーク
Pages: 336 (272 in Color)　￥16,000
An effective logo is the key to brand or company recognition. This sourcebook of total CI design introduces pieces created for a wide range of businesses - from boutiques to multinationals - and features hundreds of design concepts and applications.

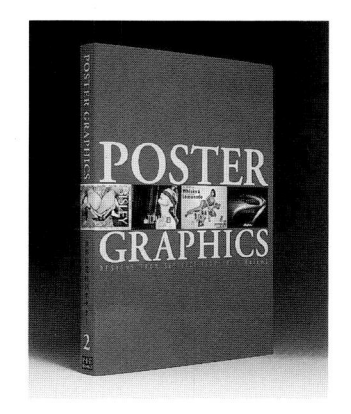

POSTER GRAPHICS Vol. 2
好評！業種別世界のポスター集大成、第2弾
Pages: 256 (192 in Color)　￥17,000
700 posters from the top creators in Japan and abroad are showcased in this book - classified by business. This invaluable reference makes it easy to compare design trends among various industries and corporations.

BROCHURE & PAMPHLET COLLECTION Vol. 4
好評！業種別カタログ・コレクション、第4弾
Pages: 224 (Full Color)　￥16,000
The fourth volume in our popular "Brochure & Pamphlet" series. Twelve types of businesses are represented through artwork that really sells. This book conveys a sense of what's happening right now in the catalog design scene. A must for all creators.

BROCHURE DESIGN FORUM Vol. 2
世界の最新カタログ・コレクション
Pages: 224 (176 in Color)　￥16,000
A special edition of our "Brochure & Pamphlet Collection" featuring 250 choice pieces that represent 70 types of businesses and are classified by business for handy reference. A compendium of the design scene at a glance.

A CATALOGUE AND PAMPHLET COLLECTION
業種別商品カタログ特集／ソフトカバー
Pages: 224 (Full Color)　￥3,800
A collection of the world's most outstanding brochures, catalogs and leaflets classified by industry such as fashion, restaurants, music, interiors and sports goods. Presenting each piece in detail from cover to inside. This title is an indispensable sourcebook for all graphic designers and CI professionals.

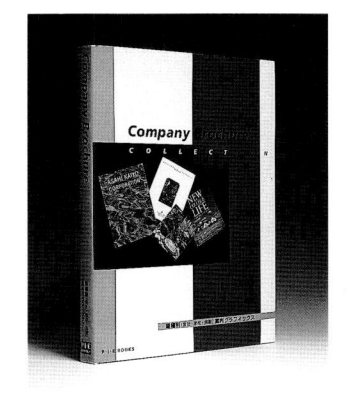

COMPANY BROCHURE COLLECTION
業種別（会社・学校・施設）案内グラフィックス
Pages: 224 (192 in Color)　￥16,000
A rare selection of brochures and catalogs ranging from admission manuals for colleges and universities, to amusement facility and hotel guidebooks, to corporate and organization profiles. The entries are classified by industry for easy reference.

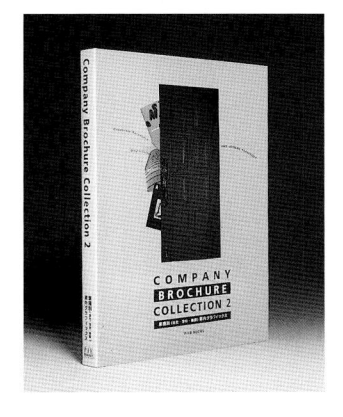

COMPANY BROCHURE COLLECTION Vol. 2
業種別会社案内グラフィックス　第2弾！
Pages: 224 (Full Color)　￥16,000
Showing imaginative layouts that present information clearly in limited space, and design that effectively enhances corporate identity, this volume will prove to be an essential source book for graphic design work of the future.

CORPORATE PROFILE GRAPHICS
世界の会社案内グラフィックス
Pages: 224 (Full Color)　￥16,000
A new version of our popular "Brochure and Pamphlet Collection" series featuring 200 carefully selected catalogs from around the world. A substantial variety of school brochures, company profiles and facility information is offered.

CREATIVE FLYER GRAPHICS Vol. 2
世界のフライヤーデザイン傑作選
Pages: 224 (Full Color)　￥16,000
A pack of some 600 flyers and leaflets incorporating information from a variety of events including exhibitions, movies, plays, concerts, live entertainment and club events, as well as foods, cosmetics, electrical merchandise and travel packages.

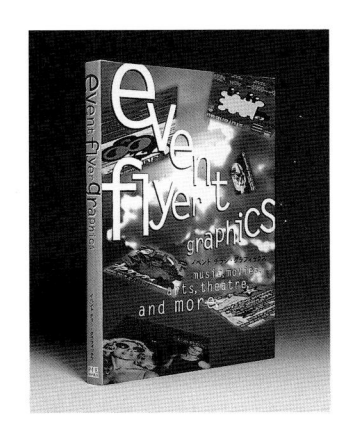

EVENT FLYER GRAPHICS
世界のイベントフライヤー・コレクション
Pages: 224 (Full Color)　￥16,000
Here's a special selection zooming in on flyers promoting events. This upbeat selection covers wide-ranging music events, as well as movies, exhibitions and the performing arts.

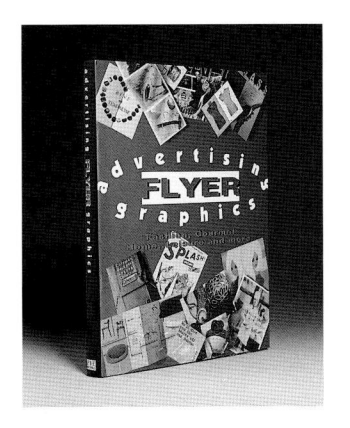

ADVERTISING FLYER GRAPHICS
衣・食・住・遊の商品チラシ特集
Pages: 224 (Full Color)　￥16,000
The eye-catching flyers selected for this new collection represent a broad spectrum of businesses, and are presented in a loose classification covering four essential areas of modern lifestyles: fashion, dining, home and leisure.

CALENDAR GRAPHICS Vol. 2
好評カレンダー・デザイン集の決定版、第2弾
Pages: 224 (192 in Color)　￥16,000
The second volume of our popular "Calendar Graphics" features designs from about 250 1994 and 1995 calendars from around the world. A rare collection including those on the market as well as exclusive corporate PR calendars.

THE P·I·E COLLECTION

DIAGRAM GRAPHICS Vol. 2
世界のダイアグラム・デザインの集大成
Pages: 224 (192 in Color)　¥16,000
The unsurpassed second volume in our "Diagram Graphics" series is now complete, thanks to cooperation from artists around the world. It features graphs, charts and maps created for various media.

NEW TYPO GRAPHICS
世界の最新タイポグラフィ・コレクション
Pages: 224 (192 in Color)　¥16,000
Uncompromising in its approach to typographic design, this collection includes 350 samples of only the very finest works available. This special collection is a compendium of all that is exciting along the leading edge of typographic creativity today.

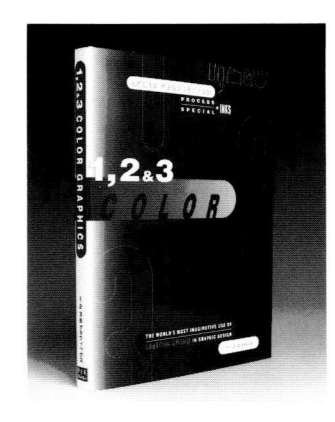

1, 2 & 3 COLOR GRAPHICS
1·2·3色グラフィックス
Pages: 208 (Full Color)　¥16,000
Featured here are outstanding graphics in limited colors. See about 300 samples of 1,2 & 3-color artwork that are so expressive they often surpass the impact of full four-color reproductions. This is a very important book that will expand the possibilities of your design work in the future.

1, 2 & 3 COLOR GRAPHICS Vol. 2
1·2·3色グラフィックス、第2弾
Pages: 224 (Full Color)　¥16,000
Even more ambitious in scale than the first volume, this second collection of graphics displays the unique talents of graphic designers who work with limited colors. An essential reference guide to effective, low-cost designing.

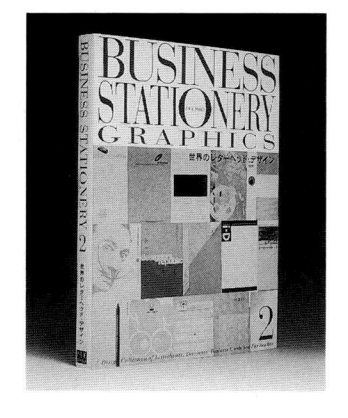

BUSINESS STATIONERY GRAPHICS Vol. 2
世界のレターヘッド・コレクション、第2弾
Pages: 224 (176 in Color)　¥16,000
The second volume in our popular "Business Stationery Graphics" series. This publication focuses on letterheads, envelopes and business cards, all classified by business. Our collection will serve artists and business people well.

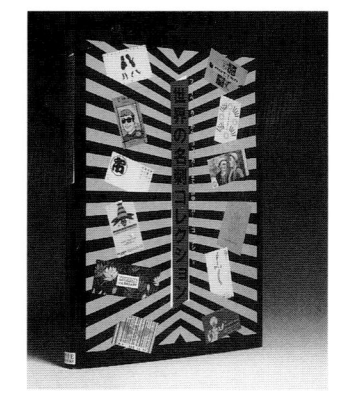

BUSINESS CARD GRAPHICS Vol. 1 / Soft Jacket
世界の名刺コレクション／ソフトカバー
Pages: 224 (160 in Color)　¥3,800
First impressions of an individual or company are often shaped by their business cards. The 1,200 corporate and personal-use business cards shown here illustrate the design strategies of 500 top Japanese, American and European designers. PIE's most popular book.

NEW BUSINESS CARD GRAPHICS
最新版！ビジネスカード グラフィックス
Pages: 224 (Full Color)　¥16,000
A selection of 900 samples representing the works of top designers worldwide. Covering the broadest spectrum of business categories, this selection of the world's best business cards ranges from the trendiest to the most classy and includes highly original examples along the way.

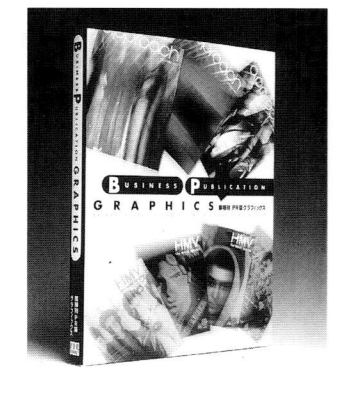

BUSINESS PUBLICATION GRAPHICS
業種別企業ＰＲ誌・フリーペーパーの集大成！
Pages: 224 (Full Color)　¥16,000
This comprehensive graphic book introduces business publications created for a variety of business needs, including promotions from boutiques and department stores, exclusive clubs, local communities and company newsletters.

POSTCARD GRAPHICS Vol. 4
世界の業種別ポストカード・コレクション
Pages: 224 (192 in Color)　¥16,000
Our popular "Postcard Graphics" series has been revamped for "Postcard Graphics Vol. 4." This first volume of the new version showcases approximately 1,000 pieces ranging from direct mailers to private greeting cards, selected from the best around the world.

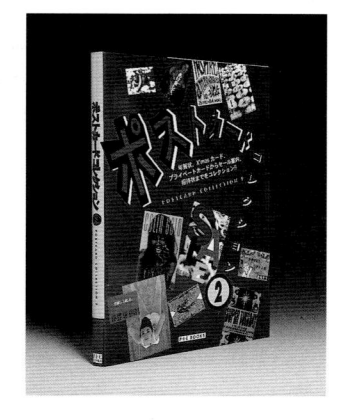

POSTCARD COLLECTION Vol. 2
ポストカードコレクション／ソフトカバー
Pages: 230 (Full Color)　¥3,800
Welcome to the colorful world of postcards with 1200 postcards created by artists from all over the world classified according to the business of the client.

TRAVEL & LEISURE GRAPHICS
ホテル＆旅行 案内 グラフィックス
Pages: 224 (Full Color)　¥16,000
A giant collection of some 400 pamphlets, posters and direct mailings exclusively delivered for hotels, inns, resort tours and amusement facilities.

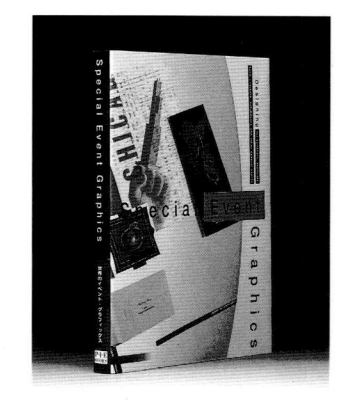

SPECIAL EVENT GRAPHICS
世界のイベント・グラフィックス
Pages: 224 (192 in Color)　¥16,000
A showcase for event graphics, introducing leaflets for exhibitions, fashion shows, all sorts of sales promotional campaigns, posters, premiums and actual installation scenes from events around the world. An invaluable and inspirational resource book, unique in the world of graphic publishing.

THE P·I·E COLLECTION

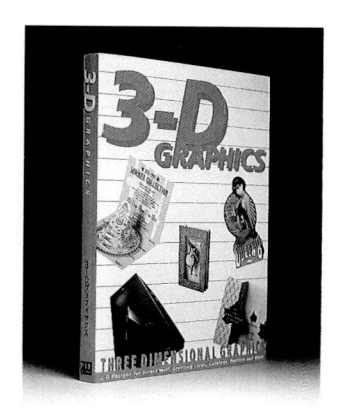

3-D GRAPHICS
3Dグラフィックスの大百科
Pages: 224 (192 in Color)　¥16,000
350 works that demonstrate some of the finest examples of 3-D graphic methods, including DMs, catalogs, posters, POPs and more. The volume is a virtual encyclopedia of 3-D graphics.

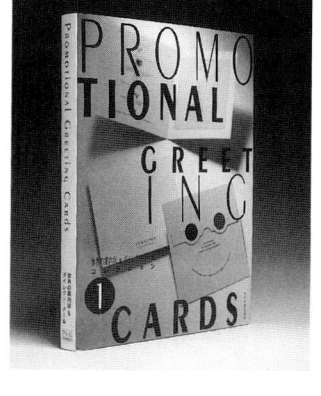

PROMOTIONAL GREETING CARDS
ADVERTISING GREETING CARDS Vol. 4
(English Title)
厳選された世界の案内状＆DM
Pages: 224 (Full Color)　¥16,000
A total of 500 examples of cards from designers around the world. A whole spectrum of stylish and inspirational cards, are classified by function for easy reference.

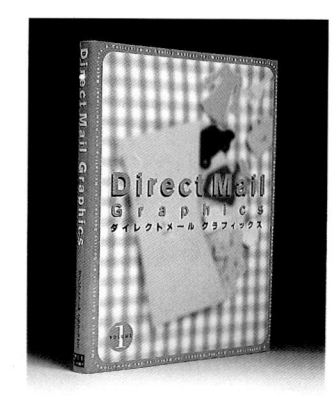

DIRECT MAIL GRAPHICS Vol. 1
衣・食・住のセールスDM特集
Pages: 224 (Full Color)　¥16,000
The long-awaited design collection featuring direct mailers with outstanding sales impact and quality design. 350 of the best pieces, classified into 100 business categories. A veritable textbook of current direct-marketing design.

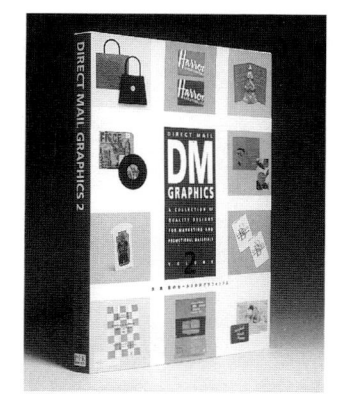

DIRECT MAIL GRAPHICS Vol. 2
好評！衣・食・住のセールスDM特集！第2弾
Pages: 224 (Full Color)　¥16,000
The second volume in our extremely popular "Direct Mail Graphics" series features a whole range of direct mailers for various purposes; from commercial announcements to seasonal greetings and are also classified by industry.

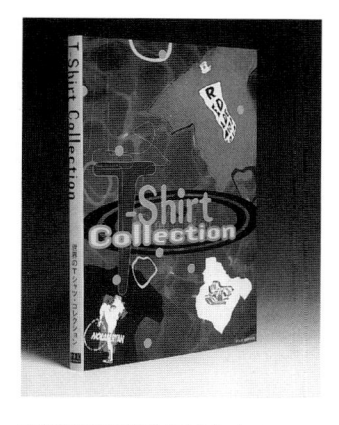

T-SHIRT GRAPHICS / Soft Jacket
世界のTシャツ・コレクション／ソフトカバー
Pages: 224 (192 in Color)　¥3,800
This stunning showcase publication features about 700 T-shirts collected from the major international design centers. Includes various promotional shirts and fabulous designs from the fashion world and sporting-goods manufacturers as well. This eagerly awaited publication has arrived at just the right time.

T-SHIRT PRINT DESIGNS & LOGOS
世界のTシャツ・プリント デザイン＆ロゴ
Pages: 224 (192 in Color)　¥16,000
Second volume of our popular "T-shirt Graphics" series. In this publication, 800 designs for T-shirt graphics, including many trademarks and logotypes are showcased. The world's top designers in the field are featured.

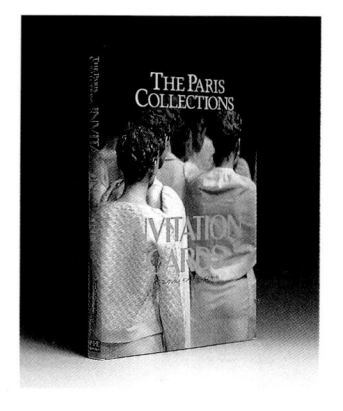

The Paris Collections / INVITATION CARDS
パリ・コレクションの招待状グラフィックス
Pages: 176 (Full Color)　¥13,800
This book features 400 announcements for and invitations to the Paris Collections, produced by the world's top names in fashion over the past 10 years. A treasure trove of ideas and pure fun to browse through.

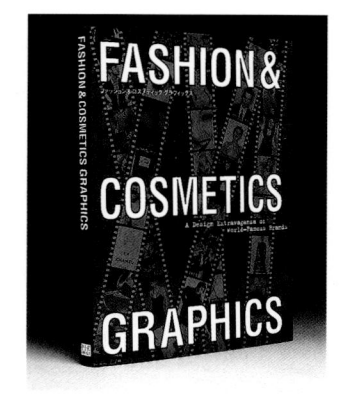

FASHION & COSMETICS GRAPHICS
ファッション＆コスメティック・グラフィックス
Pages: 208 (Full Color)　¥16,000
A collection of promotional graphics from around the world produced for apparel, accessory and cosmetic brands at the avant-garde of the fashion industry. 40 brands featured in this book point the way toward future trends in advertising.

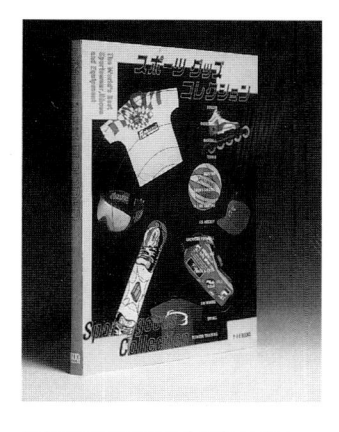

SPORTS GRAPHICS / Soft Jacket
世界のスポーツグッズ・コレクション／ソフトカバー
Pages: 224 (192 in Color)　¥3,800
A collection of 1,000 bold sporting-goods graphic works from all over the world. A wide variety of goods are shown, including uniforms, bags, shoes and other gear. Covers all sorts of sports: basketball, skiing, surfing and many, many more.

LABELS AND TAGS COLLECTION Vol. 1 / Soft Jaket
ラベル＆タグ・コレクション／ソフトカバー
Pages: 224 (192 in Color)　¥3,800
Nowhere is brand recognition more important than in Japan. Here is a collection of 1,600 labels and tags from Japan's 450 top fashion names with page after page of women's and men's clothing and sportswear designs.

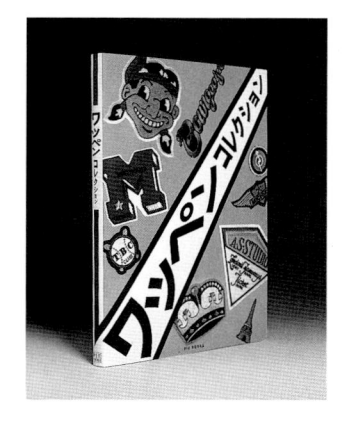

INSIGNIA COLLECTION
ワッペン＆エンブレム・コレクション／ソフトカバー
Pages: 224 (Full Color)　¥3,800
Over 3000 designs were scrutinized for this collection of 1000 outstanding emblems and embroidered motifs that are visually exciting, make innovative use of materials and compliment the fashions with which they are worn.

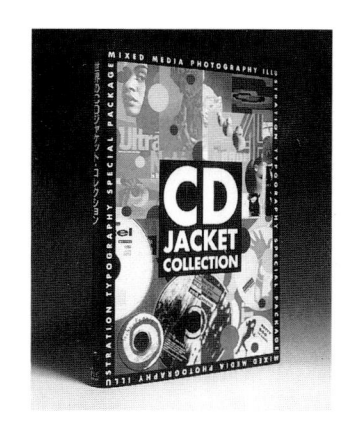

CD JACKET COLLECTION
世界のCDジャケット・コレクション／ソフトカバー
Pages: 224 (192 in Color)　¥3,800
Featuring 700 of the world's most imaginative CD and LP covers from all musical genres, this is a must-have book for all design and music professionals.

THE P·I·E COLLECTION

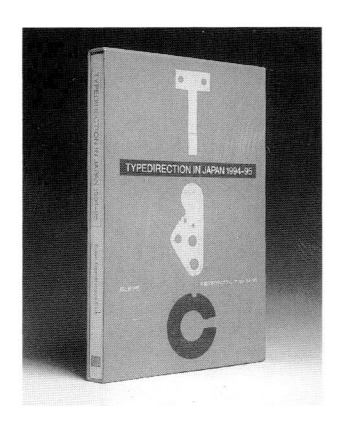

TYPO-DIRECTION IN JAPAN Vol. 6
年鑑 日本のタイポディレクション '94-'95
Pages: 250 (Full Color)　¥17,000
This book features the finest work from the international competition of graphic design in Japan. The sixth volume of our popular yearbook series is edited by the TOKYO TYPE DIRECTORS CLUB with the participation of master designers worldwide.

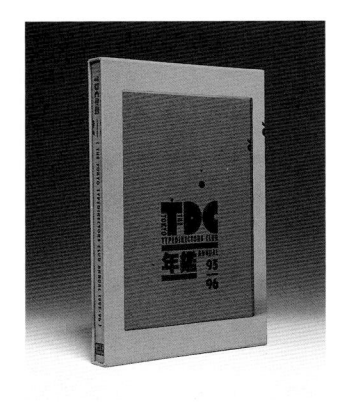

THE TOKYO TYPEDIRECTORS CLUB ANNUAL 1995-96
TDC 年鑑95-96
Pages: 250 (Full Color)　¥17,000
A follow-up publication to Japan's only international graphic design competition. Featuring 650 typographic artworks selected by THE TOKYO TYPEDIRECTORS CLUB, this book provides a window on the latest typographic design concepts worldwide.

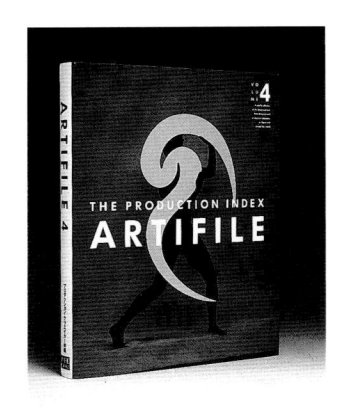

The Production Index ARTIFILE Vol. 4
活躍中！広告プロダクション年鑑、第4弾
Pages: 224 (Full Color)　¥12,500
The fourth volume in our "Production Index Artifile" series features vigorously selected yearly artworks from 107 outstanding production companies and artists in Japan. An invaluable source book of the current design forefronts portraying their policies and backgrounds.

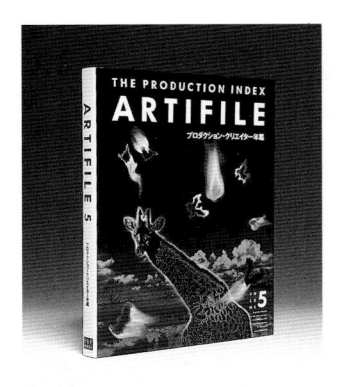

The Production Index ARTIFILE Vol.5
最新版プロダクション・クリエーター年鑑
Pages: 224(Full Color)　¥12,500
ARTIFILE 5 features artwork from a total of 100 top Japanese production companies and designers, along with company data and messages from the creators. An invaluable information source for anyone who needs to keep up with the latest developments in the graphic scene.

SEASONAL CAMPAIGN GRAPHICS
デパート・ショップのキャンペーン広告特集
Pages: 224 (Full Color)　¥16,000
A spirited collection of quality graphics for sales campaigns planned around the four seasons and Christmas, St. Valentines Day and the Japanese gift-giving seasons, as well as for store openings, anniversaries, and similar events.

SHOPPING BAG GRAPHICS
世界の最新ショッピング・バッグデザイン集
Pages: 224 (Full Color)　¥16,000
Over 500 samples of the latest and best of the world's shopping bag design from a wide selection of retail businesses! This volume features a selection of shopping bags originating in Tokyo, NY, LA, London, Paris, Milan and other major cities worldwide, and presented here in a useful business classification.

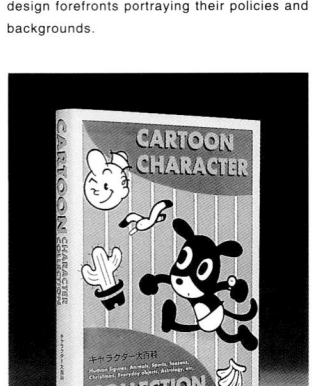

CARTOON CHARACTER COLLECTION
5500種のキャラクターデザイン大百科
Pages: 480 (B&W)　¥9,800
A total of 5,500 cartoons and illustrations from some of the most successful illustrations in the industry have been carefully selected for this giant, new collection. The illustrations included are classified by animals, figures, vehicles, etc, for easy reference.

カタログ・新刊のご案内について
総合カタログ、新刊案内をご希望の方は、はさみ込みのアンケートはがきをご返送いただくか、90円切手同封の上、ピエ・ブックス宛お申し込み下さい。

CATALOGUES ET INFORMATIONS SUR LES NOUVELLES PUBLICATIONS
Si vous désirez recevoir un exemplaire gratuit de notre catalogue général ou des détails sur nos nouvelles publications, veuillez compléter la carte réponse incluse et nous la retourner par courrier ou par fax.

CATALOGS and INFORMATION ON NEW PUBLICATIONS
If you would like to receive a free copy of our general catalog or details of our new publications, please fill out the enclosed postcard and return it to us by mail or fax.

CATALOGE und INFORMATIONEN ÜBER NEUE TITLE
Wenn Sie unseren Gesamtkatalog oder Detailinformationen über unsere neuen Titel wünschen, fullen Sie bitte die beigefügte Postkarte aus und schicken Sie sie uns per Post oder Fax.

ピエ・ブックス
〒170 東京都豊島区駒込 4-14-6-301
TEL: 03-3940-8302　FAX: 03-3576-7361

P·I·E BOOKS
#301, 4-14-6, Komagome, Toshima-ku, Tokyo 170 JAPAN
TEL: 813-3940-8302　FAX: 813-3576-7361

804 Helge D. Rieder
Lassallestraße 61
51065 Köln